RUNDOWN

Robert Auletta

I0139523

BROADWAY PLAY PUBLISHING INC
New York
www.broadwayplaypub.com
info@broadwayplaypub.com

RUNDOWN
© Copyright 1981, 1982, 2004 Robert Auletta

First edition: February 2018
I S B N: 978-0-88145-768-1

First published by B P P I in *Plays By Robert Auletta* in September 2004

Book design: Marie Donovan
Page make-up: Adobe Indesign
Typeface: Palatino

RUNDOWN was produced by Robert Brustein at
the American Repertory Theater in Cambridge,
Massachusetts, from 13 April through 9 May 1982. The
cast and creative contributors were:

PAY .... Stephen Rowe
SPEAR .... Tony Shalhoub
LAURE .... Karen Macdonald *or* Marianne Owen
TRACER .... Thomas Derrah

Director .... Bill Foeller
Set design .... Kate Edmunds
Costumes .... Nancy Thun
Lighting .... James F Ingalls
Sound .... Stephen Drury

RUNDOWN was then performed in Israel during A R T's summer 1982 European Tour. It was scheduled to be performed in several Communist block European countries before reaching Israel, but was withdrawn from these performances because the State Department, who had sponsored the first part of the tour, believed that the play was "Critical of the Vietnam war and of certain aspects of American life." Robert Brustein argued that it was important to show these countries that America was open to self criticism. Needless to say, the State Department's view prevailed.

After the American Repertory Theater production, RUNDOWN was produced, with a somewhat different cast, at Judson Church in New York City on 13 January 1983.

RUNDOWN was cited by the American Theater Critics Association as one of the ten best plays produced outside of New York City during the 1981-82 season.

The play was revised in November 2003

CHARACTERS & SETTING

PAY, *a recently returned Vietnam vet*
SPEAR, *an old friend of* PAY's
TRACER, *a cohort of* SPEAR's
LAURE, *an old friend of both* PAY *and* SPEAR

Time: late Spring 1973

Place: New York City

ACT ONE

(Darkness. Now some light appears. Dawn. We see PAY *huddled in a chair, a blanket around him. We hear the static-ridden sounds of a radio: popular music, some garbled words, more music.* PAY *shifts around in his chair. Suddenly he stiffens, as if seeing something. Vaguely we make out a form standing on the other side of the room.)*

PAY: What? Who's there? Do you want me?

(Silence. The lights fade out. Darkness. After a while the lights come back up. Bright, cheerful, a fine day. Pay is on his feet, smiling. He addresses the audience.)

PAY: It was a beautiful day. An amazing day. I decided that I would go over to my mother's house. I hadn't seen her for a while. *(He takes a few steps, stops, looks around, smiles.)* I certainly enjoy this kind of weather. All of a sudden everything seems filled with possibilities. Bursting *(He begins to walk, bright, snappy; then suddenly, He stops, looks around, a bit dismayed)* Sometimes too many possibilities, if you know what I mean. I'm sure you've felt that way yourself at times, a bit overwhelmed.

(We hear the sound of a radio: a news commentator, a frantic D J, static, a rock song, static. PAY *now realizes that it is* SPEAR'*s voice that he's hearing.)*

SPEAR: *(V O)* Hey, Pay! Where the hell are you, man? You know that I've been looking high and low for you. Of course, you do, 'ol pal. I mean, why not tune an ear

to 'ol Paul Revere? He's waking up the populace! He's
anticipating the Apocalypse! *(He starts to sing.)*
He's busting up the megalopolis!
Searching through the static of the city,
Soon the two of us will be sittin' pretty.
You can't stop it, or even try and top it—
So why not just, just just just—
Be bop it!
Bop bop bop bop—BOPPPPPP ITTTTTTT!
Just bop it, man. Just bop it, dude.
Just bop it, Pay. Just bop bop bop bop bop it!
Just go on and say, hey, I'm just gonna....

(The words and music break up. Static, silence. Throughout
PAY *has retained a slight smile on his face, betraying no*
emotion.)

PAY: Well, as I was saying, better get on over to my
mom's. No use hanging around wasting time.

(The radio: an operatic tenor begins to sing something
plaintive. PAY *listens a bit, then begins to mime singing*
along with the tenor; then static. Now we hear SPEAR's
voice, once more.)

SPEAR: *(V O)* Come on, Pay. No bullshit. Listen to me.
Time is running out. For both of us. So let's just…

*(*PAY *makes a violent cut-off gesture with his hand. The*
voice makes a gurgling sound. Static, silence)

PAY: *(To the audience)* Too much bullshit out on the
airwaves these days. Every dog having his day, it seems.

(A dog is heard howling in the distance.)

PAY: With the dog catcher never around when you
need him. Of course, you know what they do to those
mutts after they catch them. *(He starts to walk; a slight*
smile on his face. After a few steps, he stops.) You might
not have guessed it, but I'm a successful person. In fact,
in some people's eyes, I'm a very successful person.

I guess that's why I don't get over to my mother's as often as I would like—preoccupied as I am with my business ventures. *(He looks around.)* The city looks great, but there does seem to be something strange about it. I mean, things just don't seem to be in their right place. Have you noticed or is just me? *(The radio: jazz, an upbeat sound)* I love music. I...

SPEAR: *(V O)* Come on, Pay. Stop jacking off! Walk to me, straight to me. You'll find me. Trust your instincts, my man!

PAY: *(Slight smile)* Fuck you. *(Static, silence; looking around. To the audience)* Actually, buildings seem to be involved. Major building having been moved about during the night. *(Smiles)* You see, I've been trying for over an hour to get on the road to my mom's, but it seems my visual references have been deceiving me. Time for a cup of coffee.

(PAY walks over to a table, sits down, picks up a cup of coffee and begins to drink. After a few moments TRACER enters. He watches PAY for a while and then walks over to his table. PAY looks up. An operatic tenor begins to sing. PAY begins to mime singing along with the singer. TRACER stands to the side imitating him. The music stops.)

TRACER: *(Walks over to the table where PAY is sitting.)* Do you mind if I sit here?

PAY: Why should I care?

TRACER: Thanks. *(He sits down.)* Beautiful day, isn't it?

PAY: Haven't noticed.

TRACER: I'm starved, though. How's the food here?

PAY: It's dog food. *(Smiles)* Great if you're an animal.

TRACER: You know what they do with those dogs when they catch them, don't you? The ones without a license, I'm talking about.

PAY: I have no idea.

TRACER: *(He makes a loud "shussssh-ing" sound.)* It's not a pretty situation you're facing, if you're a non-conforming, freedom loving canine, with a devil-may-care attitude, and a rampant sense of social responsibility—which some may label irresponsibility—depending on their political makeup, and what kind of sex they had the night before, if any—if you know what I mean?

PAY: I can't say I do.

TRACER: Fascism running amok, soon they'll cart you away in a truck.

PAY: You're a poet?

TRACER: Not exactly. But I do have a Longfellow between my legs! *(He laughs uproariously.)*

PAY: I think I heard that one back in the fourth grade. *(He flashes his dead smile and turns away from him.)*

(Radio: opera, a duet, a man and a woman. Static, silence, then SPEAR's voice.)

SPEAR: *(V O)* Hey, Pay, remember how we used to love kidding around with your father's opera collection! We'd go down to the basement with the old seventy-eights and… *(He begins to sing opera, something comic; then static, silence)*

PAY: *(To himself)* I remember.

TRACER: What did you say?

PAY: Nothing. I'm basically a non-speaker.

TRACER: But you must have heard something. I mean, it sounded like you were responding to someone.

PAY: I heard you.

TRACER: No. Someone other.

PAY: There is no other.

TRACER: Then I must be just plain crazy, I guess.

PAY: I would say so. *(He starts to get up.)*

TRACER: Hey, what's up, friend? Why so agitated? What's the big hurry?

PAY: I'm off. Gotta run some errands.

TRACER: On a day like today?

PAY: That's the combination: me and today.

TRACER: *(Laughs)* You'll never make it!

PAY: But I'm a crazy fucker. Nothing can stop me once I get started.

TRACER: But they've changed things around. Haven't you heard? Last night. Buildings were involved. Sacred landmarks. Roads, even—doubling back on themselves or disappearing into the void. It was a sudden whim of the city administration, I'm told. Personally I'm appalled.

PAY: *(Laughs strangely)* Someone's fucking with my mind.

TRACER: Meeeeee?

PAY: Yeah, you mother…

TRACER: Listen, it's better if you quiet down, lie low, listen to old friends. And before you know it, what's broken shall be mended. And the lame and the halt shall once more play stickball.

PAY: Spear must have hit rock bottom, hanging out with dog-shit liar like you.

TRACER: Hey, hey you just watch your….

(PAY looks like he is about to hit TRACER.)

TRACER: Okay, okay. *(He smiles.)* But before you explode, could you loan me eight dollars and seventy-five cents?

PAY: What for?

TRACER: To make a long distance phone call.

PAY: Up yours.

TRACER: It's really important.

PAY: Reverse the charges.

TRACER: I wasn't brought up that way.

PAY: Who are you going to call?

TRACER: What?

PAY: Somebody I know?

TRACER: Somebody you know?

PAY: Yeah. Keep him informed about my whereabouts?

TRACER: If you wantta know the truth, it's an old friend in New Delhi.

PAY: New Delhi?

TRACER: Yeah. New Delhi, Arkansas! An old friend just opened a brand new deli in Arkansas! *(He laughs wildly.)* I'm the type who likes to stay in touch. And not just with friends of mine—but with friends of friends, even.

PAY: It was a pleasure, it really was.

(PAY starts to leave but TRACER grabs him by the arm.)

TRACER: *(Viciously)* Give me eight dollars and seventy-five cents! And from your heart!

PAY: I give nothing.

(PAY and TRACER begin struggling.)

TRACER: The thing is, I don't simply want it from your pocket, but straight from your god-damned heart!

PAY: That's the one place that I never give from—ever! Anymore!

TRACER: *(Laughing)* Well, learn, soldier, learn.

PAY: *(His strength seems to give out)* What did you call me?

TRACER: I called you "soldier." *(He is holding* PAY *securely now.)* I thought you were tough, soldier. What's happened to you?

PAY: *(Vaguely)* I don't know. Things. Vicissitudes.

TRACER: Sorry, I don't speak French.

PAY: You might want to learn. It's a beautiful language.

TRACER: Language of love, they say.

*(*TRACER *lets go of* PAY.*)*

PAY: Yeah. The problem is, I just don't love anybody, anymore. I mean, outside a certain family member or two.

TRACER: That's too bad. I love everybody.

PAY: I just want to be left alone. No love, no interference, no meaningful encunters.

TRACER: You said a bad word.

PAY: What? *(Thinking about what he said)* Yeah. I guess you're right. I did. I apologize to all concerned.

TRACER: You have a dirty mind.

PAY: I used to, but not anymore. All that's gone now. Everything scrubbed clean. Dirt, grime. All the interesting stuff down the drain. I'm left with the taste of antiseptic in my mouth.

*(*PAY *takes out money and gives it to him.* TRACER *gives him the change.)*

TRACER: You know what? This is going to go straight into the fund.

PAY: What fund you talking about?

TRACER: Why, that very special fund dedicated to the purification of almost all currently existing systems.

PAY: So you think most systems need purifying?

TRACER: Of course they do. They're foul. They're filthy. The very air is deteriorating. Any right-minded person can see that. Look. *(He breathes in deeply, then begins to cough violently.)*

PAY: You probably exaggerate a bit.

TRACER: Not me. Once I peed blood.

PAY: You've probably got a bad bladder.

TRACER: Not me. I've got an exceptional bladder, if the truth be known. I get down on my knees every day.

PAY: To pee?

TRACER: No. To thank God, for what He has given me, soldier.

PAY: I've got a discharge, you know, an honorable, an honorable... You understand.

TRACER: *(Laughing wildly)* And I'll bet you earned it too! I'll bet you made your country proud! Fields littered with your handiwork!

PAY: I... *(He stops.)*

TRACER: Maybe you haven't peed enough blood yet— heart's blood, I mean, in order to know the truth about yourself. But soon I think you'll be ready.

PAY: For what?

TRACER: For a radical readjustment and purification of all currently existing circumstances! That's what!

PAY: You tell Spear...

TRACER: *(Interrupting him)* What? Who?

PAY: Spear, Spear!

TRACER: You lost your little spear?

PAY: You tell him, I see him... Forget it. *(Pause)* Nowhere near the heart.

TRACER: What?

PAY: That money I gave you!

TRACER: Where did it come from, then?

PAY: From my ass, buddy! From my ass!

TRACER: *(Starts to exits, then stops)* It's not a dog.

PAY: What?

TRACER: What you heard howling out there. It's not a dog at all. It's a wolf doing the howling, my friend. A big bad wolf.

(PAY turns, walks a bit, then stops. TRACER exits into the darkness. PAY addresses the audience.)

PAY: One thing you have to realize: I'm not here to tell you the truth. I'm not here to lie either, but I have lied recently. Remember when I said that I was a successful person? Well, it's not true at all. Not by anybody's standards. *(He begins to whistle while he walks across the stage. Finally he stops by a bench in front of a railing down by the river.)* Yes, it was truly a beautiful day. I was down by the river. I was a sailboat. My sails filled with the breezes of spring.

(Radio: A soprano sings, lonely, beautiful. PAY listens. The sound fades. He sits down on the bench and closes his eyes. LAURE enters and goes over to the railing facing the water. He opens his eyes and sees her. He betrays no emotion as he addresses the audience.)

PAY: Have you ever noticed how much people resemble each other these days? How certain types seem to shadow us throughout our lives, dog us?

(LAURE turns and looks at PAY. She betrays no emotion.)

LAURE: Were you speaking to me?

PAY: Not at all.

LAURE: It sounded like you were speaking to me.

PAY: Actually, I wasn't speaking.

LAURE: It sounded like you were.

PAY: Well, then I must be crazy. Have you considered that fact?

LAURE: Not yet.

PAY: Well, consider it.

LAURE: I will.

(Pause)

PAY: Well, how's it going?

LAURE: What?

PAY: The fact you're considering.

LAURE: Fine. It's coming along just fine.

PAY: Have you reached a conclusion?

LAURE: No, I haven't.

PAY: You seem to be a successful type person.

LAURE: Yes.

PAY: It shows.

LAURE: Thank you.

PAY: I'm not complimenting you.

LAURE: No?

PAY: Not at all. That wasn't a compliment at all. Actually it was the total opposite of a compliment.

LAURE: Fine.

PAY: You probably work and play with a group of upper-uppers, of leaders. That sort.

LAURE: Yes, as a matter of fact, I do—on occasion, anyway.

PAY: Well, you'd probably be surprised how many of them are maladjusted.

LAURE: Would I?

PAY: Sure. Probably about ninety percent of them, at any given moment: bats. And I'm not just talking bats in the belfry, but batted right out of the fucking ballpark!

LAURE: I'll bet.

PAY: They just don't show it, that's all. Their hallmark being, hypocrisy; their savvy, staying in power. So then tell me, why is it that we're always so eager to please them, to do whatever they tell us to do—even though, deep down, we know that it's just a crock of shit— empty illusions created by a group of lunatics in order to keep themselves in power?

LAURE: We don't always do what they want.

PAY: No? Just most of the time. And that's because we're sheep! Acres and herds and fields of ba-ba sheep—both black and white—sheep being driven to the slaughter.

LAURE: You know, I don't much buy that sheep idea of yours. Little too easy, I think.

PAY: Oh, yeah. Then why not try and come up with something on your own, if you're so smart?

LAURE: Maybe you're right? Maybe I should try, if I'm so smart—though I'm not so sure I am.

PAY: And to make it interesting, why not bet your ass on it?

LAURE: Bet my ass on it?

PAY: Yeah, bet that, and I'll bet you'll win. Believe me.

LAURE: Not necessarily.

PAY: No? Why not?

LAURE: Because I've bet it in the past, and I've never actually won. Not what I really wanted, anyway.

PAY: You're got to be kidding?

LAURE: No, I'm not kidding.

PAY: Your ass? Your ass on the line? I mean, how can you lose with that kind of motivation behind you?

LAURE: Is that supposed to be joke?

PAY: I'm not sure. What do you think?

LAURE: You know what I think: I think no matter how motivated you are, you can still lose—and I mean decisively.

PAY: Well, congratulations. To lose decisively takes guts. And who knows, keep it up long enough—betting your ass and all—and you just might turn out to be a big winner.

LAURE: Who knows?

PAY: And you know why? Because everything about you spells WINNER to me; maybe a little incognito, maybe still a little shy—but, sooner or later, BIG WINNER, as far as I'm concerned.

LAURE: Maybe on a superficial level—but no other.

PAY: But I thought you started off saying that you were the successful type, hanging out with upper-uppers, leaders, movers/shakers, whatever?

LAURE: I believe you said or implied most of that, not me.

PAY: Come on. Own up. You said or implied a little bit yourself.

LAURE: Not as emphatically as you.

PAY: Still, is it true, or not—more or less?

LAURE: More or less, yes. But… (*She stops.*)

PAY: So what's the big problem?

LAURE: Sometimes all of it, the whole package, myself included, makes me want to puke; makes me hate the fact that I'm a woman, possessing the power to conceive a human life—because the idea that this is the best I can do, the most I can accomplish with my existence, seems unacceptable—repugnant!

PAY: So I guess, you're the sensitive type. A tortured soul or something. But do you know what, nobody gives a fuck! Nobody cares! Nobody's interested! So why not just keep it to yourself?

LAURE: You're rude! Do you know that? Much ruder than you need to be.

PAY: How the hell would you know how rude I need to be?

LAURE: Maybe I have an instinct for things like that.

PAY: And maybe you don't. *(Staring off into the distance)* You know, I had a point to make, but I was sidetracked.

LAURE: Well, go on and make your point.

PAY: You know all those lunatics we've been talking about?

LAURE: I think so.

PAY: Well, they're crazy, sure: but not as crazy as me.

LAURE: No?

PAY: Not a one.

LAURE: Then what makes you….

PAY: Crazier?

LAURE: Yes.

PAY: It's the burning and screaming that does it, the burning and screaming that puts me miles and miles out in front of those bozos. You know how it is: there you are, weeks, months later, who knows?—having

a get together with a few of your good buddies—
hanging out in some well appointed R and R kind of
place—a couple of whores circulating—you know
the scene—everybody downing Buds and smoking
homegrown weed—not a care in the world—when all
of a sudden the burning and screaming comes back
to the max! —full force with everything flaming!—
and in a horrible way, it's kind of entertaining—like
Hollywood or something. But it's not Hollywood, not
Hollywood at all. With its celluloid flames… Its smell
of popcorn… Not like that at all. With its flames and
smell, sickening—like your soul, like the world around
you. And no lovers in the balcony—because all the
lovers are dead!

LAURE: Pay…

PAY: Don't Pay me! Don't name me! Don't speak to
me! This is not my world! I'm a migrant worker from
another dimension! Wherever I go, I'm in intimate
contact with the mother ship. All I have to do is give
the word, and they're on the job! Ready to suck me up,
rinse me out, administer a quick re-coup—then shoot
me back down here, forcing me to go through it all
over again!

LAURE: Then go, Pay! Contact them. Even if it's only for
a short while—just go!

PAY: Yes. Nice talking to you. You're right. I must go
my merry way now. So if you'll excuse me… (*He starts
to get up, but can't seem to make any headway.*)

LAURE: Pay… Just a second or two. (*Reaching out
towards him*)

PAY: I'm sorry. But I think I've exhausted the pleasures
of our conversation. So now…

LAURE: Pay, Pay…

PAY: What? What are you saying?

LAURE: I'm saying… *(She touches his face.)* I think I'd like to take my dress off. Is that okay? Do you mind? It's a crazy whim of mine. You see, you're not the only crazy person on the premises.

PAY: Why should I mind? I was about to close my eyes anyway.

LAURE: How come?

PAY: Need a little nap, before I go over to my mother's house. *(He sits back down on the bench and closes his eyes.)*

LAURE: Your mother's? Do you see her often?

PAY: Not as much as I should, I'm afraid.

LAURE: Well, give her my best. *(She starts to unzip her dress.)*

PAY: *(Opening his eyes)* Wait. Listen.

LAURE: What?

PAY: *(Closes his eyes, again)* I think maybe you should quit that dress removal business

LAURE: Why?

PAY: Because if you continue there's a good chance you might be, be, be… *(Stops)*

LAURE: What? Hurt in some way? Endangered? Catch a bad cold?

PAY: Yeah. Those things. That's what I mean. Who knows what evil lurks, what evil jerks…. *(Stops)*

LAURE: Yes. It's a problem. But somehow, I think, I have to take the chance. Or I should, anyway—since it's more relaxing, being unencumbered.

PAY: Yes, of course.

(LAURE removes her dress and places it on the back of the bench. She is wearing a white slip with blue embroidery)

PAY: *(Eyes shut)* You're wearing a white slip with pretty blue embroidery on it.

LAURE: Oh, I can't trust you. You peeked.

PAY: I don't need to peek when it comes to you.

LAURE: Oh no?

PAY: Because I can easily imagine whatever it is you're wearing. *(He opens his eyes and looks at her.)* Jeezzz! I was blind the whole time. I swear go God. But I still saw the truth of your underwear. *(Staring)* I hate to see you like this, you know. For various reasons.

LAURE: Don't worry. We'll talk. Just talk, for a while. Nothing else..

PAY: Talk about what?

LAURE: What's it like for you now.

PAY: I'm back.

LAURE: I know. But what's it like?

PAY: It's like nothing. Exactly like nothing. That's the north and south of it.

LAURE: What about the east and west of it?

PAY: Those two places hold no interest for me.

LAURE: Why's that?

PAY: You see, I don't want to stretch out. What I want to do is go high, very very high or maybe low, very very low. Or sometimes both ways at once—being the sum of my aspirations.

LAURE: And what was it like there, Pay?

PAY: Like television. Just like you saw on television. Except I was inside the television set. I was trapped inside…it. Tripping over the bloody tubes and wires. Trying to hide, But I couldn't quite. Because everybody saw me, you know. Maybe you saw me? But how

could you tell for sure? We all looked alike, didn't we?
All doing the same kinds of things.

LAURE: And how do you feel now?

PAY: More or less the same. Except now I seem
to be inside some kind of television studio—with
little cameras poking into my heart and soul—and
everything cold, and antiseptic, and homeless...

LAURE: Things are changing, Pay. Important things are
happening. You can change too, if you want to.

PAY: *(Suddenly furious)* I've already changed! How
much fucking changing do you want me to do, lady!

LAURE: You can do it again. Go back to who you were.
You...

PAY: Go back to who I was? Give me a break! Thank
God I've finally left that pathetic, retread behind! What
I am now is the sum-total-truth of my ignorant and
violent nature! But the interesting thing is, I'm getting
used to it.

LAURE: You deserve better, Pay. You really do.

PAY: I'm afraid nobody is asking for your opinion.

LAURE: But there are things going on, Pay. Seismic
shifts in our society. New ways to understad—ways to
get out of the traps we've set for ourselves. To...

PAY: You've been seeing him, haven't you?

LAURE: What?

PAY: You heard me. He's been around. You've been
talking together.

LAURE: Listen, Pay...

PAY: *(Furious, interrupting her)* Don't bullshit me, Laure!
I don't need that from you right now. The fact is, I
don't think I need anything from you right now; so
don't push it And put your dress back on.

LAURE: All right. We don't have to talk about these things now, but...

PAY: *(Cutting her off)* But you want to, don't you? You want to try and reach me somehow! The two of you've been conniving, is the truth. He's back. There's no doubt about it. He's working the scene. He's working my head. I get these strange calls in the middle of the night, messages on the radio, notes. His handiwork. I'd recognize it anywhere. *(He laughs, stops.)* He's got people working with him too; fucked up characters you can't believe. I'm not making this up. I think he wants to get the Runaway Boys together again. Can you believe it?

LAURE: Yes, I can.

PAY: Don't you understand? I gotta be left alone— being an unreliable type, unable to deal successfully with reality. He's wanted by the F B I.

LAURE: They're a bunch of idiots.

PAY: Who cares what they are. Is he any better? They deserve each other. Anything we had between us is gone.

LAURE: He's on to something.

PAY: Oh, yeah! Onto me and various other absurd targets! And let me tell you something, Laure: it would be wise, for all concerned, for you to help keep us apart.

LAURE: We can save lives! We can make a difference. There are things to be done. And he's got the talent to do them! He's not evil, Pay, he's...outrageous and daring, but not evil. He's our old friend! Remember? *(Shivers)* I'm cold.

PAY: Put your dress on.

LAURE: I don't think it'll help.

PAY: Where are you cold?

LAURE: Especially?

PAY: Yes, especially cold.

LAURE: My thighs.

PAY: Inner or outer?

LAURE: Inner.

PAY: Strange. They should be among the warmest...
parts.

LAURE: I would think so.

PAY: But they're not?

LAURE: Not at all.

PAY: Do you want me to warm you, Laure?

LAURE: *(Softly)* I don't know, Pay.

PAY: Let's just see. For a moment.

*(PAY goes to LAURE and takes her hand, and leads her over
to the bench.)*

PAY: Okay?

LAURE: Yes. *(She sits down.)*

*(Now PAY kneels down before LAURE and gently opens her
legs.)*

LAURE: Pay?

(PAY takes out a cigarette lighter and lights it.)

LAURE: Pay!

PAY: This ought'a do the job.

LAURE: *(Slight laugh)* I guess.

PAY: Be able to concentrate enough warmth.

LAURE: Go ahead, then. Do it.

(He holds the flame between her thighs.)

PAY: I have to have a steady hand. I have to be able to keep my cool in order to make you hot.

LAURE: It feels good. You've found the proper distance it, seems. You've warmed me, successfully warmed me. And I'm thankful, I'm very…

PAY: I… *(Suddenly he stands up, flicking off the lighter.)*

LAURE: Why did you stop?

PAY: I lost interest. It just flagged; came to a halt. *(Staring off into the distance)* The fire has been put out, I'm afraid.

LAURE: Then light my cigarette—to make amends.

PAY: You don't seem to be smoking.

LAURE: Please, don't let that stop you.

PAY: All right.

(LAURE leans her head back. PAY lights his lighter and brings it close to her face.)

PAY: Is it lit?

LAURE: No. Not yet.

PAY: Keep puffing.

LAURE: I am.

PAY: Are you sure you're puffing?

LAURE: Yes, like crazy! Yes!

(PAY pulls the lighter away, extinguishing the flame.)

LAURE: You shouldn't have stopped…so soon.

PAY: And you shouldn't play with fire.

LAURE: He is back, Pay! Like you, Pay! What do you expect!? Both of you together! Think of it! You were his best friend! Of course he wants to see you. The two of you have a lot to talk about.

PAY: You keep this up, you're going to end up burning down the house.

LAURE: I almost made the Runaway Boys, didn't I?

PAY: Not quite.

LAURE: A couple of times I came close. Very close.

PAY: You'd always chicken out at the last minute.

LAURE: It's harder for a girl, Pay. It's more difficult. Trickier. Come on. *(She gets up.)* Let's go

PAY: What? What are you doing?

LAURE: Let's go to the river, Pay. Let's go look at the river. Play with the river. Tease it with our desires.

(LAURE climbs over the fence and stands by the river. PAY does the same.)

LAURE: I'm not so much of a chicken anymore, Pay. You'll see. *(She goes over to the edge.)* It's running fast. It looks dangerous.

PAY: Can't get out of the city fast enough. Heading into the ocean. It wants to forget itself. It wants to forget everything. It wants to become the ocean. It holds no allegiance to the land. No attachment. I know what it's about. I understand its desires.

LAURE: Yes, yes. We both understand. *(She begins walking on the edge of the embankment.)*

PAY: Laure?

LAURE: It tempts, it tempts. It makes you want to show your stuff. It makes you want to show your naked stuff.

PAY: Laure, let me tell you something, it doesn't matter if you're brave, it doesn't help. In fact, I think it makes things worse.

LAURE: No. I think you're wrong. I think it's what's needed. Especially now.

PAY: If that's what you want.

(PAY *grabs* LAURE'*s arm, then pushes her partly out over the edge, while at the same time holding onto the railing with the other hand.*)

LAURE: *(Crying out)* Pay!

PAY: I could drop you, couldn't I?

LAURE: Yes!

PAY: I could drop both of us, couldn't I? First you, then me.

LAURE: Yes, you could.

PAY: Then sooner or later we'd both go invisible. Under the water, under the bridges, then out to sea. Becoming the sea itself.

LAURE: Do whatever you have to, Pay.

PAY: *(Fiercely)* Is that what you want, Laure? What you really want?

LAURE: Maybe. Maybe! Maybe's not good enough? You're still a chicken, Laure! Chicken to the gristle! Chicken to the bone! Chicken, chicken, chicken! Chicken go home!

(PAY *pulls* LAURE *back. We can't tell if she's laughing or crying.*)

LAURE: I'm not a chicken, Pay! I just think, that's all! I just try and think! And sometimes it's hard to think hard! Painful to think about life and death, and all that lies in between! And then to act on it! To act on what you believe in a decisive manner!

PAY: It makes no difference, if you're brave or not, if you think or not! So give up and go home! And tell your buddy, I'll bust him good if he continues to haunt me!

(The lighting begins to change. PAY *walks away from* LAURE. *The sound of sea gulls crying out.)*

*(*LAURE *and* PAY *are in different spaces now—each surrounded by darkness.)*

LAURE: I'm alone in my apartment. It's night. I hear you, Pay. I hear what you're saying.

PAY: Midnight in the heart of the stone.

LAURE: In the heart of America.

PAY: Midnight in the heart of the stone. I saw this little boy, he was just sitting there, expressionless, holding his severed leg in his arms. Kind of cradling it, rocking it a back and forth, like it was a Teddy Bear, his favorite toy. Sweet child.

LAURE: Midnight in the heart of America.

PAY: But I had to run by. There was a wall of fire coming down the road behind me. I couldn't look back. I had to run by.

LAURE: We'll change it, Pay, the heart of America.

PAY: No! The Runaway Boys have been finished, Laure. Finished. Rundown. They can't do anything. Nothing, nothing.

LAURE: No, Pay! Wait for me, Pay! *(She turns and runs into the darkness looking for him.)*

PAY: Not a chance. *(He turns away.)*

(Darkness. The lights comes back up on PAY. *Midmorning. He glances back at the river, then addresses the audience.)*

PAY: I was over at the O T B the other day and ran into my friend Wendell. He was messed up pretty bad in World War Two, lost his left hand, and a few other key parts of his personal environment. But does he let it get him down? No, sir. Whenever the Blues starts to do a number inside his head, he wraps his remaining hand around a pint of what-the-doctor-ordered, a concoction known as blackberry flavored brandy, and downs it—like a kid with a bottle of Coke on a sweltering August day. I mean, he definitely knows how to attack the root of his sorrow: the brain. *(He smiles wanly and begins to look around.)* You see, I was trying to get to my mother's house, but somehow I kept finding myself going around in circles, kept finding myself down by the river, running into certain…undesirables.

(SPEAR enters. He is wearing a Groucho nose and glasses. He moves along the rail, looking out at the river, his back to PAY.)

SPEAR: It's a beautiful day.

PAY: *(With some fear)* What did you say?

SPEAR: I said, it's a beautiful day.

PAY: *(Turning and looking at him now.)* You must be thinking of some other day.

SPEAR: You mean a day from the far flung past, or perhaps something waiting in the vertiginous future?

PAY: Hey pal, don't ever ever use that V word in front of me again! Okay? It's disgusting!

SPEAR: You mean specifically disgusting?

PAY: Yes. You see, what I hate most in life are pretentious assholes going around showing off their vocabularies! It's demeaning to be forced to listen to words that one-does-not-understand! It makes me absolutely insane to be around a person who bombards me with stuff like that.

SPEAR: Gee whiz. Well, sorry, I guess then, golly, that I'm just a pretentious, show-off'ey kind'a guy. But I didn't think there was any real harm to it. I mean….

PAY: Well, there is fucking real harm to it! So grow up and face reality!

SPEAR: *(Staring at him)* What's the matter? You don't look good. Are you sick, or something?

PAY: In a banana of speaking, I am.

SPEAR: So it seems you ate a bad banana?

PAY: It seems I did; perhaps somewhere along the line someone slipped me a bad banana—laced with some sort of dangerous substance, and foolish me, like a dope, swallowed it.

SPEAR: Perchance someone slipped it to you on a porpoise?

PAY: Perchance a porpoise, perhaps a porpoise. But maybe an untrustworthy baboon did the dirty work? How the hell should I know? Most of the time I'm asleep at the wheel.

SPEAR: You know what, kid, I hate to tell you, but it seems you've been the victim of some kind of vicious subterfuge— believing that you were getting a wholesome banana and all—but instead they took you for a ride! They took you for a sucker and slipped you a Mickey! Shanghaied you and dropped you into a world of endless pain, not to mention shit!

PAY: Well, that's your theory. That's the way you look at it.

SPEAR: And what's your theory?

PAY: I don't have theories. I'm not rich or intelligent enough to have theories. I just do what people tell me to do. That's the way I'm programmed. You know that guy Jerkoff, with the rats?

SPEAR: Who?

PAY: Jerkoff, the Russian guy, learned how to program rats.

SPEAR: Pavlov, you mean.

PAY: Could be. Anyway, this guy figured out ways to get them to do whatever he wanted them to—made them contort, fight, salivate, fuck, tap dance, play pinochle, whatever. Societies love that idea, embracing it as the eleventh commandment. Man is not such a lost cause after all, it proves—if you can make him do what you want him to do without him knowing he's been setup.

SPEAR: Sounds like you, well, dig that idea a little bit yourself?

PAY: Tell me, bro, what's America supposed to do with the thousands and thousands and thousands of baby rats that it produces each year—let them run wild? Do anything they please? Rape, rob, pillage, steal— screw their moms, kill their dads— avoid the draft because they're afraid of the big boom boom noise? Of course scientific people had to start messing with their brains—fooling with them way back when, in the ancient days of the potty seat—so when the time comes to roll out the thunder, they'd be able to put a fucking team together!

SPEAR: But who do you believe in? I mean, when push comes to shove, the rat in you, or the man?

PAY: Me? What can I tell you? For better or worse, I'm just a grown up, programmed rat.

SPEAR: Alas, old chum, you were once a prime primate, a great free ranging beast! King of the Hill! Lord of all he surveyed! One of the legendary Runaway Boys! But now, unfortunately, poisoned and defaced, led into the jungle and left there to rot in sickness and disgrace.

(SPEAR *removes the glasses and looks at* PAY.)

PAY: You know, you look better with those things on.

SPEAR: A lot of people have been telling me that lately. (*He starts laughing.*) Hey, Pay, come on! You're back, and I'm setting up shop! I mean, what else is happening down that blind alley of yours? We can hang out and shoot the breeze. What's to lose? We'll have some yucks.

PAY: No.

SPEAR: Come on. You know we always knew how to have fun together. That's all I'm talking about.

PAY: No.

SPEAR: You know, it's hard to argue with that "no" of yours.

PAY: Yes, it is.

SPEAR: Come on, Pay. Give me a big hug and a kiss!

PAY: I don't go around hugging and kissing strange men.

SPEAR: You think I'm strange?

PAY: You're weird, man.

SPEAR: Nah. I'm just an average Joe passerby.

PAY: You're not a jogger?

SPEAR: Do I look like a jogger?

PAY: Maybe under those clothes you've got a little jogger outfit on.

SPEAR: *(Checking his clothes)* Don't seem to.

PAY: Too bad.

SPEAR: You like joggers?

PAY: Not so much. But somehow I'm taken by the idea of what you could accomplish if you were a jogger.

SPEAR: What exactly?

PAY: You could jog yourself to death.

SPEAR: Could I?

PAY: Definitely. I mean, you'd have to work hard at it. It might take a long time, hundreds of miles and all. But I know you're not afraid of discipline and hard work. And it would be a good death: clean, healthy, outdoorsy—as far as deaths go these days.

SPEAR: And how do deaths go these days?

PAY: Some are quite bad.

SPEAR: I'll bet.

PAY: Like this guy I heard about disemboweled... A jagged piece of bamboo in his guts... A million miles from nowhere... His weapon out of reach... It could take a long time... Ouch, ouch he must have kept saying... Oooooo, he must have kept saying... For hours, days. Unless the animals got to him first.

SPEAR: We gotta talk, Pay.

PAY: No, man. Not us. Ta ta. *(He starts to exit.)*

SPEAR: Where are you heading?

PAY: Over to my mom's.

SPEAR: Oh. I see. Well, give her my regards.

PAY: You must be kidding.

SPEAR: No. Why do you think so?

PAY: *(Laughs)* She'd have you arrested. She'd turn you in.

SPEAR: Oh, I don't think she'd do that.

PAY: A lot of people would like to do that to you, Spear.

SPEAR: Not your mom.

PAY: Some people would, like to see you swing.

SPEAR: Not you.

PAY: Who knows...nowadays?

SPEAR: What do you mean?

PAY: You know, guys like me who fought the beast—
getting a couple of quarts of blood outta guys like you,
who found a way out—might be just what the doctor
ordered.

SPEAR: I did some stuff too, Pay. Don't forget.

PAY: Tell it to the Marines.

SPEAR: We were always fighters, both of us. Always
taking on the local bullies! Remember the fun of
it? Two, we discovered, being mathematically and
physically superior to one. Ask that big bully Weegee.
Remember the day we took care of him? I'll bet his
balls are still ringing!

PAY: *(In spite of himself being pulled back into the past.)*
There's something else I remember real well.

SPEAR: What's that?

PAY: That frosty morning when you stole that pint of
cream off my mother's porch and drank it behind the
bushes. Boy, was she pissed.

SPEAR: It was good cream.

PAY: *(A yell)* Jezzzzzussss!

(PAY and SPEAR rush to one another and embrace.)

PAY: I don't know why I'm saying it, but it's good to
see you again.

SPEAR: You made it home, Pay. That's what's
important.

PAY: Not exactly home anymore, somehow. *(He pulls
away.)* Sorry. I gotta take off now. Lots of pressing
meetings. presidents and potentates, not to mention the
boys down at the O T B, who have come to recognize
me as some sort of a sage.

SPEAR: What's it like, Pay, getting back and all.

PAY: When I first got back I hung around with some heavy hitters, drug users, you know. I thought it was a good idea, maybe become some kind of addict myself. But it didn't happen. So I was left out in the cold. Not even an addiction to keep me company.

SPEAR: Are you working? Got anything going for yourself?

PAY: Actually, I have a great job. I work at home on the telephone. People call me. We have chats. My job is to assume the guise of various well known cartoon characters. Elmer Fudd is a big favorite, but basically I do them all. Bugs, Donald, Heckel, Jeckel, Tweetie Bird, Mr McGoo… People love it.

SPEAR: You know, you're still as zany as they come.

PAY: *(With some real feeling.)* That's me! What I truly am! A comical personality! Always trying to see the funny side. The little absurdities. The wackado moments. The whoppee cushion, the exploding cigarette, the joy buzzer, the dribble glass, the pack of gum that practically snaps your fucking finger off. The endless yucks that make life worth living!

SPEAR: So hang out with me, man.

PAY: I like the way you say that. Real easy.

SPEAR: It is easy. Like it was in the old days.

PAY: The old days are all used up.

SPEAR: No. They're not. We were the Runaway Boys! We had the magic. As soon as we get back together again, it'll come back. All we want. All we can use. I promise you.

PAY: 'Fraid not.

SPEAR: Listen, Pay: God wants us to be extravagant in our desires.

PAY: God? I thought you didn't believe in God?

SPEAR: I don't. I only believe in the idea of God, what
He would want "if" He existed; what He would
desire "if" He was really calling the shots. And what
He'd do, I'm sure, is drive our asses to moon rock
and back! And without the luxury of rocket or space
capsule! Forcing us to employ nothing but our own
considerable resources, in order to change our view of
the world!

PAY: If any God whatsoever, is on duty, in any way
whatsoever—I'm sure to fucking positively certain that
He wakes up each morning with a blinding migraine,
and one thought fixed in His mind, that being: Today's
the day that I'm going to totally annihilate this entire
group of aimless, savage, worthless, destructive,
monkey-brained fucks—that in a fit of weakness, I once
created and deigned to call my own! And you know
what, I don't give a damn about that famous promise I
once made about restraining myself—because I'm God
and I can do whatever I god-damned well please!

SPEAR: Then why hasn't He done it?

PAY: Because He's addled brained! Always putting
the ultimate act off, for whatever stupid reason. But
wait a little bit longer. You'll see. One day He'll follow
through, and it'll be spectacular.

SPEAR: Listen, Pay. The thing is, I've been working
with a few guys like you. Most of them are coming
along fine, starting to see all kinds of interesting new
possibilities. Give it a try. What do you got to lose?

PAY: You know, what it is, Spear? I think there's some
kind of lie twisted up inside you.

SPEAR: You really think so?

PAY: Yes, I do. I don't know exactly what it is, but it's
there—snaking around your heart. It's always been
there, I think.

SPEAR: Are you saying you never trusted me?

PAY: No. What it is, what it was—I trusted you enough, but never entirely.

SPEAR: That's a shocking thing for an old friend to hear. It really is. But...hey! Let's look at the bright side. This could be our golden opportunity!

PAY: What opportunity?

SPEAR: For me to show you, you were wrong! *(He pulls two bandannas out of his pocket.)* So, come on.

PAY: What?

SPEAR: *(Throwing him a bandanna)* Let's test it.

PAY: Test what?

SPEAR: The old Runaway Boy magic! The old Runaway Boy truth! I'll show you that it still works. Still exists. Trust me. First I'll go and then you. *(He ties the bandanna around his head, covering his eyes.)* A lot of traffic out there today, isn't there?

PAY: Holy shit! You're not going to...

SPEAR: *(He spins around a couple of times.)* Now do me a favor and point me into the thick of things, will you, Pay?

(PAY points him.)

SPEAR: Then follow me. Will you do that for me?

PAY: You know, you're going to end up in a hospital. Or worse.

SPEAR: Not me! Not only am I honest, but will—I promise you—not end up in any hospital! Worse, possibly; but a hospital, never! The Runaway Boys! We've got the magic! *(He runs into the traffic.)* The Runaway Boys!

(The lighting changes. Darkness, headlights, the sound of brakes squealing, voices cursing)

VOICE: Hey, you goddamn psycho!

SPEAR: Up yours, Daddy Cool!

VOICE: You oughtta be locked up!

SPEAR: With your mama!

VOICE: Fuck you, Jack!

SPEAR: Do it to your mama!

VOICE: Psycho!

SPEAR: Come on, Pay! Follow me, Pay! Trust me! The Runaway Boys! The Runaway Boys are running again!

(Darkness. Some light comes up. PAY wanders a bit. Now he goes over to a chair and sits down. There is a shadowy figure sitting in the darkness opposite him; possibly a psychiatrist.)

PAY: There was this vet named Callahan, I knew as a kid. He got himself half blinded and blown up pretty bad in Korea. I used to go out with his daughter—everybody called her Suze. Cute little Irish face. He had a terrible temper. Sometimes he'd just freak out, and if he got his hands on Suze or his old lady, he'd beat the daylights out of them. One afternoon I went over to see her. She came out of the house; didn't want me to go in. Her face was really messed up. Her father had gone nuts this time. Did even worse to her mother. I held her in my arms for a long time. I was about fifteen or sixteen. I said, I was gonna kill him. I didn't really mean it. It was just kid talk. Actually, I was terrified of the guy. But she must have believed me. Leave him alone, she said. He's too damned unhappy. Too bad off. Killing would be going easy on him. I hear him at nights. It's what he deserves. *(Pause)* I eventually lost contact with the family. It was only recently that I found out what happened to them. Seems that the mother didn't stick around very long—went off with another guy. The daughter, though, stuck with her father, right up until a couple of years ago, when Callahan finally decided he had had it, and turned his old Buick into a canister of carbon monoxide. Poor Suze didn't last two months, before she got hold of one of his old K-War souvenirs and blew her brains out. I sometimes think of those years they spent together. Maybe in some strange way they were happy, abandoned as they were by the entire world? Maybe their mutual anger somehow justified the pain of it all? I mean, it was all they had, wasn't it?—each other's pain and misery—all they could rely upon. So what was Suze to do when she lost the other half of her team?

FIGURE: Perhaps it was a stupid mistake?

PAY: *(Jumping to his feet)* What? What did you say? *(There is a shiver up and down his back. The voice sounds familiar to him.)*

FIGURE: What's the point of wasting your life, when there are so many more interesting alternatives?

PAY: What? I don't know. I don't know anything, when you get down to it. Nothing at all! So don't fucking ask me! Whoever you are!

(Darkness. The lights come up. PAY *is looking out at the audience.)*

PAY: Have I told you anything about Laure? How I used to feel about her? It's certainly not that way anymore. I mean, even at its best, there was usually this running battle between us—both of us over-playing our roles—with her as Little Miss Do Right, hoping to find an acceptable way to go wrong, and me as Mister Go Wrong, making fun of all those that went right. But still, she always drew me to her, somehow—inspiring these crazy fantasies. You see, what it was: I wanted to comb her beautiful hair. I wanted to give her a Toni Home Permanent. I wanted to take off her shoes and paint F-U-C-K across her toenails. I wanted

us to ride naked together on twin white horses into
St. Patrick's Cathedral on Christmas Eve. I wanted to
rip off her jewelry and throw it into the arms of the
poor. I wanted to attack her values. I wanted her to fall
sobbing into my arms. I wanted to fall sobbing into her
arms. I wanted to buy her a washer-dryer combination.
I wanted her to buy me a powder blue tie and
handkerchief set, monogrammed, of course, with a pair
of gold plated cufflinks, thrown in as a sweetener. In
those days I would have crawled through hellfire just
to get a peek at her knees. *(He gets down on his hands and
knees and begins to crawl.)*

(The lights come up on LAURE. *She is sitting on a couch in
her apartment. She watches* PAY *as he crawls into the room.)*

LAURE: It's nice of you to come over.

PAY: I just happened to be in the neighborhood.

LAURE: Why don't you sit down? *(She pats the couch.)*

PAY: Does that mean I have to stand up first?

LAURE: I'm afraid it does. Do you think you can
manage it?

PAY: I'll give it a try. *(Slowly he stands up, moaning and
groaning as he does.)*

LAURE: There! You did it! You should be very proud of
yourself.

PAY: Yes. It seems, I've rejoined civilization. For a short
time, anyway. Thanks to you. *(He sits down next to
her.)* This is a nice couch. *(He bounces up and down a few
times.)* I think I'd like to have sex with it.

LAURE: Don't let me stop you.

PAY: Of course not.

LAURE: I'll go into the other room. I wouldn't want to
inhibit you. *(She starts to get up.)*

PAY: One thing.

LAURE: What?

PAY: She's not a virgin, is she?

LAURE: I don't know what she does when I'm not home.

PAY: Because I don't want the responsibility of a "first time." I don't want any complications. No strings. Understand?

LAURE: I think she'll go along with that.

PAY: Aren't you going to offer me a bonbon or something?

LAURE: How about a bonbon, Pay?

PAY: No. I despise bonbons.

LAURE: Well, in that case, how about…

(PAY *grabs* LAURE's *hand, kisses it, then stands up.*)

PAY: Well, I'm off.

LAURE: Why'd you do that?

PAY: What, stand up?

LAURE: No, kiss my hand?

PAY: Actually I was planning on biting it, but somehow my lips had other ideas.

LAURE: Please sit down, Pay.

(PAY *sits back down.*)

PAY: Hey, I've got an idea! Let's watch television!

LAURE: If you like.

PAY: What's on, war?

LAURE: On second thought—let's skip it.

PAY: That's too bad. I like keeping a tab on war. It draws you in every time. The N F L being a pale imitation. What else do I have these days? I mean, what it is, Laure... *(He is now staring intently at her.)* The sad truth of the matter: I don't think you'll ever be able to shock me again with the poetry of your presence, bring tears to my eyes with your touch, like you once did. You know what I mean?

LAURE: Don't count on it.

PAY: Why? Do you have something up your sleeve?

LAURE: Yeah. I have the past, and I have the future.

PAY: Two areas that hold no interest for me.

LAURE: I also have *me* up my sleeve. The present *me.* But perhaps the present is a little too 'iffy for you these days?

PAY: As I've said: things are no longer as they were.

LAURE: And as I said: don't count on it.

PAY: *(Looking around)* This is a real spiffy joint you have here. The money must really be rolling in.

LAURE: Tell me, have you become obsessed with money? If so, I think it's about time you get over it. I mean, do you really think it's the root cause of evil, of war, possibly? Think about it: capitalism, socialism, communism, fascism—who's innocent? Catholic or protestant, who doesn't like to draw blood? Why didn't anybody tell the French Revolution to stop lopping off all those heads? What about Africa and its endless supply of blood thirsty dictators?

PAY: You know, you're funny, Laure, chasing your tail around like that. It's very entertaining, you trying to make sense out of the world.

LAURE: *(She hisses at him like a cat.)* I've made a good living in advertising. Do you think it's evil? Do you think selling shit that doesn't live up to its hype will somehow lead us to a totalitarian state?

PAY: Lead us!?! You gotta be kidding! *(He laughs and gestures "look around".)* You really like thinking about this stuff, don't you?

LAURE: Yes, I do. But what about you? What do you think about these days, Pay?

PAY: Not much. I mean, what's there to think about, anyway. It's all up to the individual, isn't it? And I know, too well, what he's like. Basically, I'm against everything; some things a little more than others.

LAURE: Right. It's all up to individuals like us—moving forwards and backwards in time—trying to consolidate, trying to create—thought-filled, rage-filled, semi-idealistic creatures, knowing how hard it is to make any real difference, but still, still—willing to break off from the collective, willing to go forward, pursuing their individual destinies, individual desires—being, at the core, heat seeking, pleasure hunting animals, who… *(She begins moving sliding across the couch towards him. Now she presses her breast against him.)* Who, somehow know, just what they need.

PAY: Laure?

LAURE: What?

PAY: Please stop using your girl-power on me.

(LAURE and PAY's faces are very close together.)

LAURE: Why? It's nature's way of altering the status quo, of creating an entire new set of circumstances. Of bringing a little happiness to a world that desperately needs a salubrious taste of the mysterious. Little demons of pleasure being lodged in our every crevice. So why not elect to give them a field day? Just let them loose and see what happens. Oh, look! There's a few lodged in my fingertips. Wow! *(She begins to caress him.)* How do you like them? They seem to like you a lot.

(PAY *stands up.*)

PAY: Are you his lover?

LAURE: Who's? Spear's? No! I was your lover!
Remember? Never his. Don't tell me you're jealous?

PAY: I don't think so. The thing is, I just don't like
being used—which I feel may be currently happening.
You see, I have one rule and one rule only: I refuse to
be drawn into anyone else's plans.

LAURE: So then why are you here?

PAY: So I could look you in the eye and tell you: that I
refuse to be drawn into anyone else's plans.

LAURE: Society's embarrassed by men like you, Pay.
It might be smart to start looking for help in others—
even though, perish the thought, some intimacy might
result.

PAY: I don't know what's smart anymore. And I don't
very much care, or give a damn about most things you
could mention—but once in a while I see something,
well, amusing, hysterical, even—like the other day...
(*He starts to laugh.*) You should have seen him run into
traffic—as blind as a bat, and nobody hit him! He's
a maniac! Certifiable—he tried to sink a courthouse!
I read about it over there—stuck up to my waist in
Delta mud! My old childhood buddy tried to sink a
goddamned courthouse! Can you imagine? And he
wasn't so far off, they said. His calculations being
pretty good, for a guy who never studied engineering.
What lay under the damned thing was just basically
muck. The whole damned edifice literally propped up
above a swamp! Technically speaking, sinking it was a
real possibility! A larger charge might just have done
it. How could he know shit like that?

LAURE: He said he wanted to watch Justice sink slowly into the mud and disappear—forcing us to rethink the whole concept.

PAY: He's a brilliant guy. Much smarter than I ever was. Speaks three languages fluently; spent a year and a half in a monastery, and doesn't believe in God! And to top it off, he killed an elephant!

LAURE: I love animals; so I felt pretty bad about that—but it got an enormous amount of attention.

PAY: To say the least! He assassinated a circus elephant nicknamed Nixon!

LAURE: Kids hated him for that; everyone hated him for that.

PAY: How the hell do you poison an elephant? What do you do, go into a hardware store and say: Hey, I've got pests I wantta get rid of. What'd ya got, the guy says, roaches, mice, rats? No, what I've got are elephants. Oh, elephants! I've got just the thing. Here, this will kill an elephant!

LAURE: They say Nixon went pretty fast; though he was a little gassy during his final hours.

(LAURE and PAY both laugh.)

PAY: Kept saying, I'm not a crook, I'm not a crook!

(LAURE and PAY continue laughing. We see SPEAR in the shadows watching them.)

LAURE: We had some great times in the old days, didn't we? Remember those kissing parties we had in the eighth grade?

PAY: Yeah, Post Office, Spin The Bottle, down in some kid's basement. The unwitting parents upstairs. Nice kids, they're thinking. They're so quiet. Do you think they're studying? Hot stuff!

LAURE: That's where I learned how to kiss—with the two of you monopolizing me for your evil purposes.

SPEAR: Yes, yes! We had her where we wanted her!

(They hear him but don't hear him.)

LAURE: Passing me back and forth like a bag of smooch candy. Could have ruined a girl's reputation. But it felt pretty good, I have to say. Wow! I still think about it.

PAY & SPEAR: You kiss her, I kiss her—You kiss her, Me kiss her—Me Kiss her, You kiss her—Kiss kiss kiss her on the kisser! *(They laugh uproariously.)*

LAURE: And then one day the unspeakable happened. *(She screeches.)* Aaaaaaaaaaaaa! Malcolm Blankenstop grabbed my breast!

PAY & SPEAR: Malcolm Blankenstop! You little weeny! That's right! Run for your life, you little skunk! Because when we catch you, we're gonna kick your runty ass! *(They laugh uproariously.)*

LAURE: You know, forever after, Malcolm was unable to look me in the eye. Every time he saw me he turned bright red and started staring at his shoes.

(SPEAR recedes into the darkness.)

PAY: They were the greatest times. Nothing so good after that—for me, anyway. You guys were different, though. Both of you did well in school. You had real futures, if you wanted them.

LAURE: You went to college.

PAY: Yeah, for a year. And then I dropped out. I could never get it together. Get focused. Fighting with my old man all the time. Moving in and moving out. Never finding anything I much liked to do. No passion, I guess. Spear was smart and passionate about injustice, though; knew how to stay focused, too; a top student. Dropped out of college in his last semester—wrote a statement saying that his leaving school should be counted as an act of political and social dissent. Went down south to help organize poor people; then later to Latin America to do, God knows what? I never knew. He was different when he came back. Who knows what he saw down there?

LAURE: Pay…

PAY: And you, you were a major smarty pants—getting a scholarship to a fancy girl's college. A history major! Everybody was impressed.

LAURE: You're as smart as anyone I know.

PAY: No, I'm not. I couldn't get jackshit together then. And just look at me now, I'm worse.

LAURE: (*Almost whispering*) It's not your fault— whatever it is. Believe me, Pay. Things happened to you that shouldn't have, even before the war. I know that, I know that. I know you so well. Believe me. Remember your poem, back in high school?

PAY: Poem?

LAURE: You couldn't get enough of it. You made me memorize it. Sometimes we recited it, like, ten times a day. It was driving me crazy! How can I ever forget it?

PAY: Gunga Din! You're right! The damned thing became an obsession with me!

(PAY *and* SPEAR *look at each other for a moment or two, then begin to recite the poem, fiercely, and with a pretty good accent.*)

PAY & SPEAR: You may talk 'o gin an' beer
When you're quartered safe out 'ere,
An' you're sent to penny-fights an' Aldershot it;
But if it comes to slaughter
You will do your work on water,
An' you'll lick the bloomin' boots of 'im that's got it.

Now in Injia's sunny clime,
Where I used to spend my time
A-servin' of 'Er Majesty the Queen,
Of all them black-faced crew
The finest man I knew
Was our regimental bhisti, Gunga Din.

It was "Din! Din! Din!
You limping lump o'brick-dust, Gunga Din!
Hi! slippy hitherao!
Water, get it! PANEE LAO!
You squidgy-nosed old idol, Gunga Din!"

PAY: Yeah! He was always there. The water boy.
Cursed and despised—eternally darting through
the gun fire, filling the helmets of the troopers with
what they most desired. And then one day, the guy
who's telling the story gets shot in the gut. And there
he is writhing in the dust, choking mad with thirst,
breathing his last, he thinks—when Din gets to him,
and gives him a pint of the green slimy stuff. But to
a wounded man, it's the best, the purest, the holiest
water on the goddamned planet! Then Din starts
pulling him to safety...

(We see SPEAR *in the shadows watching them.)*

LAURE: 'E carried me away
To where a dooli lay,
An' a bullet come an' drilled the beggar clean.
'E put me safe inside,
An'just before 'e died:
"I 'ope you liked your drink, sez Gunga Din.

PAY: So I'll meet 'im later on,
In the place where 'e is gone—
Where i's always double drill and no canteen;
'E'll be squattin' on the coals.
Givin' drink to pore damned souls,
And I'll get a swig in Hell from Gunga Din!

LAURE & PAY: Din! Din! Din!
You Lazarushian-leather Gunga Din!
Tho' I've belted you an' flayed you,
By the livin' Gawd that made you,
You're a better man than I am, Gunga Din!

(Both sobbing, they embrace and begin kissing away each other's tears.)

LAURE: Don't worry, Pay, you're a good boy. You're a good boy. And my best friend. And will always be. And now you've found your lost poem. And now...

PAY: *(Pulling back from her)* That poem ruined my life!

LAURE: What are you saying?

PAY: Ruined my fucking life, is what I'm saying! That poem did it!

SPEAR: You're right on target, Pay! That's what it did.

PAY: It's all clear to me now, hearing it again! That fucking poem did me in! I had no defenses against it! What an idiot I was to learn it.

LAURE: But, Pay! I don't understand! You loved that poem!

PAY: Yeah, it's this bad habit I have, falling in love with the wrong things. *(He turns and exits into the darkness.)*

LAURE: You can't blame us all, Pay! Please, come back. Pay... Please... Not all of us!

(The lights dim and go out.)

END OF ACT ONE

ACT TWO

(The lights come up. Early morning. PAY *is looking out at the audience. He looks bedraggled, like he has been up most of the night.)*

PAY: I know I can be a downer at times; kind of depressing, really. I used to hate people like that— would turn around, when I saw some depressing moron I knew coming at me, and go the other way. In the old days, even when I was down, my act was usually good enough to make people think different. Lately, though, it seems like I've lost that knack—a thing disappearing, like your ability to throw a curve ball. I mean, what it boils down to is, like the song: I can't get no, I can't get no… You know that song about satisfaction? *(pause)* So they assigned me this head doctor. A guy who was supposed to know his way around wackadoo heads like mine. And I tried hard to believe in him, to trust his knowledge, to… But it didn't' work out. Somewhere along the line, the terrible thing, I started to see, this terrible thing— he was mind-fucking me! Seeing that when you got down to it, he didn't much care about me or what it was I lost and was terrified I'd never find—caring only about teaching some sort of civics lesson, some code of social responsibility he felt I was too stupid to grasp on my own. And now I'm seeing another guy, someone outside the system—and, well, he's strange, I have to admit—but seems somehow to reach me in

some crazy way. Though I can't tell for sure, yet—
since its basically day to day, and night to night with
me—the only constant being like the song—you know
the song—I can't get no…I can't get no, no… The only
constant being…I can't get no, no…sat-is-fac-tion.
None, really.

(The sun starts to come up. PAY looks around.)

PAY: I was tired. I was trying to get to my mother's.
I saw an old fashioned candy store across the street
and decided to check it out. Have a rest; find some
sweetness. Like the old days. Take what I could, before
I got back on the road.

*(Darkness. The lights come up. PAY is sitting in the store.
TRACER is the waiter. He is wearing a coonskin cap. PAY
does not seem to recognize him.)*

PAY: I love it—an old fashioned candy store!

TRACER: Actually it's a Sweet Shoppe. You know,
spelled with an extra "P" and a "E" at the end. It's an
old timey thing. People love it.

PAY: You must be fucking kidding. So you're a soda
jerk in a, believe it or not, a Sweet Shoppe—with
an extra "P-E" stuck on for good measure! Well,
Hallelujah!

TRACER: I'm not a soda jerk, pal! I'm a maitre de!

PAY: Well, kiss my ass! A maitre-fucking-de to boot!

TRACER: Any more talk like that and you're out of
here, buster! This is wholesome place! Nothing but
fresh fruit and pure dairy products served here! Every
day droves of mother ducks and their darling little
ducklings leave here quacking with satisfaction!

PAY: That's just terrific! Because that's exactly why I'm
here—not that I'm a duck, or anything.

(PAY laughs. TRACER doesn't.)

PAY: It's a joke. You see, when I get very happy, which is rare these days, I sometimes find myself over-joking things, going into a kind of four-letter word, maniac situation—if you know what I mean? So I fucking apologize—more or less. *(He laughs.)*

(TRACER just stares at PAY.)

PAY: Anyway, what I really want, you see, what I desire beyond any normal reckoning is, *(pointing at the wall)*, a Banana Imperial! Mmmm, mmmm! Just the picture of it up there rings my chimes! Who cares about frosty Miss November, or dewy Miss May, or buxom Miss August frolicking in the hay. It's that Banana Imperial that's gonna do it for me today!

TRACER: Well, you're come to the right place. Our bananas are Chiquitas. *(He pronounces it with a strong Spanish accent.)*

PAY: Well, I do want the best. In fact, I demand the best. Because, you see, I have a problem achieving satisfaction—with dissatisfaction following me around like a dirty 'ol, nasty, stinking, radioactive cloud—and, hey, look at me. Are there any strings attached? Because sometimes I get the feeling that I'm the one pulling that damned cloud along.

TRACER: Stand up and hold out your arms, *s'il vous plait.*

(PAY does as he is told. TRACER takes out a pair of scissors and walks around PAY snipping invisible strings.)

TRACER: There. That should do it.

PAY: Hey, thanks. I mean that's great. I really, well, feel better. *(Waving his arms)* Unencumbered. I mean… *(He finds himself staring at TRACER's cap.)*

TRACER: Perchance is there something up yonder irking you, sir?

PAY: Irking me? No, of course not. I mean—the only thing conceivably in a position to irk me, *(He begins to laughs.)* is that fucking thing with the tail humping your head!

TRACER: Thing with a tail! Humping my head! I'm going make believe I didn't hear that! Do you know why I'm going to make believe I didn't hear that, sir?

PAY: No. Why?

TRACER: Because I wear this cap in honor of my great-great-great, etc. etc. grandfather, Davey Crockett! One of the early and truly startlingly original American heroes! Maybe you've heard of the Alamo?

PAY: Yes, I have. It's just outside of Chicago, I understand. But alas, it has been turned into a shopping mall. Now how about my Banana Imperial?

TRACER: Coming right up! Oh, nobel and trenchant, semi-stringless, sir! *(He exits and comes back immediately with a dish, a spoon and a napkin. Which he puts down rudely in front of PAY. The dish is full of water.)*

PAY: Fabulous! Just fabulous! *(He beings eating the water with a spoon.)* Mmmmm! Gosh! This is the real McCoy! Like I remembered from the old days. When we were kids. What times we had! I've been missing them lately, I think. But now…

(TRACER stands there smirking while PAY ecstatically attacks his Banana Imperial. Now PAY looks up.)

PAY: Why are you smirking at me? Didn't you ever see a man enjoying his just desserts before?

TRACER: Little soapy, your very just desserts, I think.

PAY: What? What are you saying? I mean…. *(Staring at his dish)* You rotten bastards! What did you slip me? Left over water!

TRACER: Better than that. Dish water. It seemed such a shame to waste it.

PAY: You're tearing me up! Trying to make a fool out of me! You and Davey Crockett and the rest of your certified heroes! Who the fuck do you guys think you are? Turning me into a joke! I'm not a joke! I'm just— wounded! Get it? Wounded and angry! And hungry for Banana Imperials, and all that goes with them! *(He cries out, jumps to his feet, and yanks the coonskin cap off* TRACER's *head.)*

TRACER: Hey, wait! Don't you dare! You keep your…

(PAY now begins to swing the cap around his head, causing TRACER *to start spinning also. From now on, whatever he does to the cap also happens to* TRACER*)*

PAY: This is for all of you! All who would deny a man his rightful Banana Imperials! *(He now begins smashing the cap on the table, them throws it on the floor, and begins stomping, punching, and gouging it.)*

TRACER: *(While under great duress)* You're a very violent man, you know that! Very violent! Frightening! I pity you, hopeless, violent, sir!

PAY: Don't pity me! All I want is you out of my dream! Get it, get it? Out of my dream! Get it? Davey Crock-of- bullshit! *(He begins to choke the cap.)*

(TRACER dies cackling horribly.)

PAY: *(Looks about hopeless, terrified)* But what happened to my Banana Imperial? Where is it, where the hell is it?

(Darkness. The lights come up a bit. PAY *seems stunned.)*

PAY: Everything was collapsing: light and memory, logic and forgiveness—all being sucked into a little black pit of nothingness—a bullet hole in the middle of some dead soldier's forehead. I knew that I didn't have

much time left. Only a miracle could save me. But of
course, they've been out of style for some time now.

(Darkness. The lights come up on PAY *sitting in a chair
talking to a man in the shadows)*

MAN: *(Speaking with a foreign accent, possibly German.)* It
is very serious for you now, my friend.

PAY: You don't have to tell me.

MAN: Though it was lucky for you to have killed that
coonskin man in your dream—for, with some luck, he
may have done likewise to you.

PAY: Is such a thing really possible? I mean, killing
someone in a dream?

MAN: Yes. Rare but still possible. There have been
cases.

PAY: How can you know for sure?

MAN: They leave traces, you know.

PAY: Who?

MAN: The dead, the dead! Those who perish in
their sleep, usually die as a result of some terrible
dream conflict. A war to the death with some violent
inconsolable. And most often, they leave behind them
bits and pieces for us to interpret—tell-tales telling of
their enigmatic final struggles.

PAY: Then it's only a matter of time. I'll keep dreaming
and dreaming, until one day one of those violent
inconsolables finishes me off. I'm afraid I'm a goner.

MAN: Not necessarily. There remains still some hope
for you in all this chaos.

PAY: Hope? What hope? I haven't any hope.

MAN: Do you happen to know Luis Bunnuel's *Le Chien
Andalou*?

PAY: No, I don't.

MAN: In the beginning of this surreal film of profound merit, we view the sight of a human eye being sliced open by a straight razor. Do you know what Bunnuel was trying to tell his audience with such a startling image?

PAY: No.

MAN: He is saying that in order to understand his film they must now watch it with their mind's eye, their inner eye, in other words. And that is exactly now what you are doing. Looking at the world as surrealists and madmen so often do.

PAY: But I'm not a surrealist! I don't have the job training or the inclination! But, you know what—I think could become a working madman without too much effort—I mean, if I'm not there already.

MAN: Whatever you think, do not shy away from your vision—for what it is, is the truth, strangely transformed. And this understanding, my friend, may eventually save you from those forces that seek to destroy you.

PAY: All I want to do is start looking at the world in some sort of half-way, normal way. Is that too much to ask? This visionary bullshit stuff you're talking about is only going to make things worse. But, who are you anyway? Are you a real shrink or a slipped away resident off a nearby ward?

(The lights come up slowly on the MAN. He looks something like SPEAR. His face is terribly white; his eyes darkly shadowed; he may be wearing a beard. He is holding a pipe in his hand, and wearing an old tweed jacket. PAY doesn't seem to recognize him.)

MAN: I am your best friend and your worst enemy; I am your Brother/Keeper, your Hunter/Executioner.

PAY: I don't want to hear that bullshit!

MAN: It is nothing, nothing. We are at all times all things to one another—always! The garrote and the loved one's caress, the shudder of death and the primal orgasm, the...

PAY: I don't care! I don't want to hear it! I don't want any garrotes, or caresses, or primal orgasms. I just want to, to go on back...back where...somehow I once was. *(He wants to leave but can't locate his will power.)*

MAN: I am Antonius the Hermit who died in the Theban desert in 357 A D; I am a man, and a jew, and the Virgin Mother of Jesus Christ; I am the unknown soldier; I am the centurion working the Crucifixion in order to garner some overtime compensation. What does it really matter who or what we are? It is all only a futile attempt to assuage our intolerable loneliness. *(He begins to cough. He takes out a handkerchief and wipes his mouth with it. The handkerchief is bloody.)*

PAY: Are you dying?

MAN: Yes, I am.

PAY: Then that makes two of us.

MAN: For me it is a forgone conclusion; but for you, it is not yet so certain.

PAY: What do you mean?

MAN: Because there is still a chance you could perhaps be saved from the great peril that haunts you—if only you can learn to trust the vision of your inner eye. And one important other thing... *(He stops.)*

PAY: What?

MAN: For you to remember. a secret... *(He is now staring into* PAY's *eyes, not saying a word—as if he might have suddenly changed his mind about telling him.)* If I dare say...

PAY: Well, go on. Say, say!

MAN: Soon you will find yourself engaged in a life and death struggle with a considerable demon. But there will be an angel nearby, as well. You must remember the angel; you must think of the angel in the midst of your struggle. And then you will triumph. If not, the demon will claim you for his own.

PAY: *(Starts to laugh)* Angels and demons! That's just the news I needed to hear! And I thought I was fucked up! I mean, do they actually pay you guys to dish out this insanity? *(The light starts to go down on Spear.)* Don't leave when I'm talking to you! Mr Hermit in the dessert! Mr Blessed Virgin Mary! I'm the psycho Vet, remember? Pay attention to me! Listen, don't you have any meds to hand out, any practical advice to offer? How about loaning me a hundred bucks so I can go down partying! Hey, I'll tell you what, let's have a fight? You can punch the shit out of me! And, who knows, maybe you'll get lucky and blacken my inner eye! And then I won't be forced to see out of the goddamned thing anymore! *(He laughs as he begins to leave, then crashes into a chair and almost trips over it.)* Aaaaaaa! *(He kicks it out of the away.)* Fuck them all! I can die on my own! I don't need their help! None of them!

(Darkness. It is late at night. PAY *sees* LAURE *in the distance in her apartment. She seems as if she's stoned.)*

PAY: What's she doing? She looks stoned or something. I could go there. To her. See her. Maybe even touch her. But I won't. I can't. I know she's conspiring against me. To make matters worse, the F B I is probably keeping tabs on her. And maybe on me as well. All because of him! I'd turn him in, if I could. I'd annihilate him—I swear!—if I could. There's a war between us. *(Thinking of what he has said.)* A war…between us. I… I thought I had a destination when I started out, but I seem to have lost it. I, I used to have a friend, everybody called

him Charlie Chop—his father was Chinese, his mother
Spanish—came from Chicago. We were on a patrol
together. Very quiet, very ordinary, as far as those
things go. Then there was this sound; nothing big; far
away it seemed—like a bird's wing snapping. Then
Charlie's on the ground, a bloody hole in his forehead.
And then later—the way the mind works—going on
and on: why birth, why life, why death, why him, why
not me? But there's nothing there, is there? Nothing
you can grab onto. What justification, what reason? It's
all random, all chance—with bullshit luck scoring our
every move. Am I wrong? Do you think I'm missing
something important? What did I leave out? *(Looks
around.)* I don't know where I'm going to sleep tonight.
I may be homeless. I'm not sure. I have a recollection
of a room and a bed somewhere—but offhand I don't
know where or if it's even mine. I do know there's a
park nearby. It's no big deal. I've slept in worse places.
I'll go into the trees. Nobody will see me.

*(PAY enters the darkness. The lights come back up. Morning.
He stands there, checking out his surroundings.)*

PAY: *(Looking around)* I should keep moving. Stay on
the march. Keep a low profile. Watch out for booby
traps.

(PAY goes a short distance when he hears a voice cry out…)

SPEAR: Heads up!

PAY: What?

SPEAR: Heads up!

*(A football comes flying through the air. PAY catches it.
SPEAR comes running out.)*

SPEAR: Get it back to me! Come on, come on!

(PAY throws it back to SPEAR.)

SPEAR: Ahh, you can do better than that. Put a little pepper on it.

(SPEAR *tosses it to* PAY, *who throws it back much harder than before.*)

SPEAR: That's good! Showed a little fire! Keep it up!

(PAY *and* SPEAR *run a few patterns.*)

SPEAR: That's it, that's it! Like the old days in the schoolyard playing two man touch.

(PAY *and* SPEAR *run another play or two, until* PAY *suddenly stops playing. Now* SPEAR *walks over to him.*)

SPEAR: Ahh, c'mon. We were a great fucking team! Could take on all comers all afternoon. All we need's a little practice, and we'll be back in business.

(SPEAR *puts his arm around* PAY. PAY *doesn't respond.*)

SPEAR: Hey, hotshot, gimme a smile.

(PAY *shoots a fake smile.*)

SPEAR: I mean something from the heart.

PAY: Haven't you heard? I give nothing from that organ these days.

SPEAR: Hey, Pay, geez, I can't believe it, what's happened to you. You're missing out, old buddy. O-U-T in a big way. (PAY *doesn't show any response.*) You can't keep going on in this semi-destitute fashion of yours. Sooner or later you're going to go over the edge, and then it's going to be too late. Don't you feel it?—I mean, that edge creeping up on you, getting closer and closer every day. I can see it in your eyes— the fear of the fall—knowing you can't do much about it. That, for some reason, you don't have the will, the desire, or…

(PAY *jumps on* SPEAR. *They grapple.* SPEAR *manages to push him off.*)

PAY: Come on, let's finish it right now! Okay? However you want it!

(PAY *throws a few punches which* SPEAR *manages to block.*)

SPEAR: Hey! Quit the macho stuff! I'm here to help you!

PAY: Oh, yeah? So tell me, what makes you so kind these days?

SPEAR: Because we go back a long way together. Back to the beginning of time. Our time. That place where everything began. You know, some people call it Paradise. The thing is, we really had it. Sometimes people forget important things, even great things—allowing them to slip away like ghosts. But what I'm saying is true. We were a fabulous team; a co-joined mind passing around the same bottle of coke. No way can I ever find someone like you again! And you know what? I think it's the same with you too, wise guy—whether you admit it or not. The world being a poorer place with us being separated. What do you got to lose?

PAY: A couple of guys were following me the other day. One of them looked familiar—reminding me of some slime ball I recently ran into, likes to wear a coonskin cap. I don't like people stalking me.

SPEAR: Tracer.

PAY: Whatever you wantta call him. Just call him off'a me!

SPEAR: I didn't put him on you, so how can I take him off? This seems to be something between the two of you. I'm not really a part of it.

PAY: He works for you, doesn't he? So pull his strings!

SPEAR: Nobody works for me. All we are is a loose confederation of people trying to help each other out;

and, just maybe, dish out a little social criticism, to
those willing to listen.

PAY: Give me a fucking break! You're like Che Guevera
to these guys. They do what you tell them.

SPEAR: Che Guevera? Don't make me laugh. I'm just
a clown. A nobody. A ham looking for attention. Che
Guevera? I don't even own a beret, let alone sport a
beard.

PAY: I heard a rumor that you went to Cuba. Any truth
in that?

SPEAR: It wasn't like that.

PAY: What do you mean, Cuba wasn't like Cuba? It
was like another country or something, only they
called it Cuba?

SPEAR: What I mean, is I didn't go there for anything
heavy.

PAY: So why'd you go, 'cause you wanted to learn
Salsa?

SPEAR: Actually, I did. I went for the Salsa and the
senoritas, and the rum and the cigars, and to watch
the waves beating on the walls of old Havana—and to
stand on the beach at night and look up at the stars, in
a place so close to, but so different from the U S of A.

PAY: You should'a been a travel writer.

SPEAR: Look, I'm not trying to bullshit you. Yeah,
I admire Castro and the Cubans; I admire the way
they stood up to the U S; I admire what he's done
for the people of his country—the illiterate, the poor,
the black, the sick—he's given them a new life. He's
returned them to the human race, restored their
dignity. Anything wrong with that? But, basically, I'm
just an admirer—not to mention, one of those guys
who needs to step out of the system every now-and-

again, in order to see how other folks do it. Curiosity
has always been the key to me. You were like that
once too, Pay, early on. Remember? Always getting
into something you shouldn't, because people were
always telling you: No or Don't Touch or Keep Out or
Better Not—but fuck them, you thought, I wantta see
for myself. And you did. But look at you now, trapped
and hopeless. I mean…

PAY: *(Interrupting him.)* Save your pity for the dogs that
trail after you.

SPEAR: You know, that wasn't like a really nice thing to
say.

PAY: No? Then what about the things you say to me?
Are they like really "nice" and I'm just missing the
fucking nuance?

SPEAR: I say what I say, because I'm trying to save your
goddamned life! Don't you get it?

PAY: And I say what I say because I know you're
setting me up for something that I don't want to be
involved with!

SPEAR: How do you know, Pay? How do you really
know? Because the reality of the situation is, you're
losing your grip—but somehow, because of some
inexplicable mind quirk, you seem to be the last on the
block to have figured it out.

PAY: So let ignorance be bliss. What the hell else do
have I going for me these days?

SPEAR: You were seen down by the river hanging off a
rail, just one step from going over.

PAY: Because I like the river! I like to fool around with
the river! It's my business! I knew what I was doing!
Anyway, it was Laure's idea.

SPEAR: You were alone.

PAY: I was with Laure another time!

SPEAR: Pay, your mother…

PAY: What about my mother?

SPEAR: Your mother's dead, Pay.

PAY: Oh, you're wrong on that one. Way off base on that one, amigo. You better go back an re-check your sources, because it sounds like some of Fidel's agents have been blowing smoke your way. And I'm not talking tobacco.

SPEAR: You were told. Your sister told you.

PAY: I've been told a lot of things lately—most of them being fucking lies!

SPEAR: Your mother's gone, Pay. Stop playing games!

PAY: My mother's a holy person. Don't you get it? She's always been that way. She's experienced holy apparitions. She has the power to forgive people. And when the time is right, that's exactly what she's going to do for me. So let's just leave it like that.

SPEAR: I'm afraid that the only holy person left in your life is me.

PAY: You think a lot of yourself, don't you?

SPEAR: Actually, I don't. What I think a lot of is our friendship. On that subject there's no compromise.

PAY: Yeah, you're holy all right. Whol-ly selfish, wholly manipulative… *(He starts to leave.)*

SPEAR: Hey, let's get it straight, my friend: our childhood was pure delight! Rapture on roller skates, Tom and Huck on bicycle wheels! We had it all! And now I want to recapture it! Take it on with us into the future!

PAY: Our childhood is gone. All ashes and rust. The vacant lots paved over, worked over, bricked over. We can't even go back there in our dreams. Because there's a fence around it!

SPEAR: No! It's all there! Still there! In our mind's eye! Just waiting for us to take hold of it! But first... Hey, Pay, Pay... *(He grabs his arm. Almost whispering)* Hey, Pay, let me tell you what we need to do, what the secret is... We have to go back into the fire; to retrieve what's been lost. The fire of battle, I'm talking about. One good action will do it. But, don't worry, the fire will be the healing variety. Like the wild fires we used to start in the vacant lots in the fall. Remember how beautiful they were! How wild and happy they made us feel! No one was ever really in danger—but still they scared the shit out of those people living on our hereditary land! And what fun it was to see the fire trucks come roaring in! With us standing around like a bunch of idiots watching it blaze: oh, no, Mr Fireman. We don't know who started the fire. *(He laughs.)*

PAY: *(Turning away)* Yeah, it was a kick. But...forget it.

SPEAR: Just give it a try, Pay. Then if you don't want to stick around, just go your way—no explanations needed; no grudge feelings held. I would never bullshit you. Believe me. I've been through it before. Nobody gets hurt. Here. From me to you.

(SPEAR puts something in PAY's hand. PAY looks at it. It is a grenade.)

PAY: Why the hell did you give me this?

SPEAR: So you can use it.

PAY: Use it? How?

SPEAR: I don't know how, or where, or when. But somehow I know you will come up with something interesting.

(PAY is staring at it.)

SPEAR: Yeah, it's real. Fell off a government tree. *(He steps back from* PAY *and stands there looking at him.)* It's time, Pay. Time to rock 'n roll.

PAY: How about I give it back to you?

SPEAR: Whatever.

PAY: Slightly altered.

SPEAR: So be it.

PAY: I mean… Like this.

*(*PAY *pulls the pin and tosses it to* SPEAR *who catches it, then presses it against his chest. Smiling)*

SPEAR: That's good, Pay. That's a start. A good start. Soon we'll be back in the real world together! Don't worry: rock 'n roll is here to stay! It's not a fad, man. So when you're ready, let's get down and dirty! Let's boogie!

(The lights go down on SPEAR. PAY *does not move away, but his body hunches tightly up, as he waits. Then, in the distance, a huge, though, somehow muted explosion is heard.* PAY's *eyes are closed; he is trembling.)*

PAY: I couldn't help it. I couldn't help any of it.

(The lights come up on LAURE's *apartment. It is about two A M. She is much like we saw her before. She turns around and sees* PAY *standing there.)*

LAURE: *(Smiling)* Nice to see you, Pay.

PAY: Is it really?

LAURE: Of course. I wouldn't lie to you.

PAY: No? Why not?

LAURE: Just wouldn't. Wouldn't want to, I guess.

PAY: Then maybe you have an ulterior motive or two hidden away somewhere?

LAURE: *(Smiling)* Don't think so.

PAY: You know, hidden away under the rug or in the dresser or God knows where people like you hide things these days—your panties, maybe?

LAURE: I'm afraid not.

PAY: But maybe you're not absolutely sure? I mean, you're a complicated person. All kinds of things going on with you—so much stuff you can't keep an eye on everything, can you? I mean, I'll bet you're even able to fool yourself after you get going—like on a fast track to some noble cause or another.

LAURE: You give me much too much credit, I think.

PAY: Not nearly enough.

LAURE: Maybe you're becoming a little overly suspicious? I mean, it's late and…

PAY: *(Interrupting her)* Are you stoned? Is that it? Should I cut you some slack because you're a bit zonked?

LAURE: Why so aggressive tonight, Pay?

PAY: Have patience. You'll find out. We'll get to the root of it.

LAURE: I'm working, Pay. And it's difficult, and it's hard to concentrate—staying up late every night, like I've been doing—so I take what I need to get the job done.

PAY: A very special advertising project, I suppose.

LAURE: What?

PAY: Working on something for him, I'll bet.

LAURE: No. For the world.

PAY: Wow! Isn't that great! What a big fucking deal! From Spear to the world! I'm impressed!

LAURE: Why are you so contemptuous of him? He was once your best friend. Why can't you give him the time of day? It's not right you treating him so shabbily. At times like these, we should be trying to reconnect with those we once cared about.

PAY: From Spear to the world—I'm bowled over. You're the middleman, I suppose. I wonder what my job is slated to be?

LAURE: Why not the time of day, the time of night, some time for him—something of yourself? Try it. You might be surprised by the results.

PAY: Because… *(He points to his heart.)* This thing won't let me.

LAURE: He understands what you're feeling, Pay. He really does.

PAY: To hell he does.

LAURE: Pay, you're having problems, serious problems, things you can't admit. About your mother and…

PAY: *(Cutting her off)* Listen! You don't know what I'm going through! You don't know what's happening with me! You don't have the slightest idea! So go back to your homework. I'm sorry I came around. I really am. Happy Halloween! *(He starts to leave.)*

LAURE: That's not true. We do understand. We have a good idea of what's going on with you. We…

PAY: *(Turning around and cutting her off)* We, we, we! What about you, Laure? He's sucked the life out of you, hasn't he! Taken your heart and soul for himself! But he hasn't given you the world in return, has he? Nothing but a piece of dried up old dog shit! Which you somehow view as gold!

LAURE: I don't think so.

PAY: It's true! I may be a madman, but I'm not a lunatic. There's a difference. And you, babe, you're much worse off than me—because you're nuts! Do you get it? Nuts! Because you think you're sane, going around leading your sanely successful workaday life— but at night you're his creature!

LAURE: I think you may be turning bad, Pay. I really do. There are signs showing. Your fears are taking over, coloring everything blood red.

PAY: Oh, yeah. What about purple and green? I like those colors too. And what about magenta? I mean, what the hell does magenta look like anyway?

LAURE: You've gone through too much. You've been left untended for too long. What should be healing is now festering.

PAY: Hey, none of us knows for sure—do we?—I mean, how bad off we really are. Or how bad we could become—what we might do in the midst of some extreme situation or another. We're both playing a very dangerous game. Don't you agree?

LAURE: Possibly.

PAY: Possibly? I mean, why hedge? Why not just admit you're playing a dangerous game—then ask yourself, if it's worth it, if…

LAURE: Forget it, Pay! Forget your dangerous game scenario. What I'm playing is a moral and intellectual game. A game of truth. The danger part is just not there for me. It's about integrity, about honesty. And for that reason, I'm not afraid. Fear belongs to other people, like… *(She stops.)*

PAY: What other people? You mean people like me? *(He stares at her.)* No? Won't answer? Okay. I'll tell you something, then: if you had any sense you'd be afraid. So let's go on with this game of yours. What do you say?

LAURE: What do you mean?

PAY: This truth game you said you were playing; so now play it with me. Okay?

LAURE: The two of us? I don't think so. It would turn into an argument, worse than the one we're having. The truth I'm interested in is a solitary one; not easily explainable.

PAY: Then try and make it a little more public. Shine some light on it. Like the time you took me into closet when we were like ten or eleven, and handed me a flashlight—said it was time I looked up your dress, get a picture of what girls were like. Remember?

LAURE: Not exactly.

PAY: No matter. The thing is, the Runaway Boys were always truth tellers. We really dug the idea—even if some of the truths told turned out to be hard to take. Spear and me used to battle all the time. Truth battles we called them. Sometimes they turned nasty, sometimes not. But that's what we really liked to do— fighting and thinking on our feet; seeing who would win. So why not give it a shot? Even if it ends up totaling what's left of our already shaky relationship.

LAURE: But I don't get the point, Pay. I really don't.

PAY: What point?

LAURE: Why do you think you have to do this?

PAY: Why? I'll tell you why. *(He grabs hold of her wrists.)* Because the two of you have had the pleasure of holding me under a microscope long enough!—peeling away my layers; seeing how much I could take before I went under. Stuff like that. Now it's my turn!

LAURE: I've never done anything horrible like that to you, Pay! Ever!

PAY: *(He is still holding her.)* Who knows? But I know you're buddy boy has!

LAURE: Pay, let me go!

PAY: And now I want to test you.

(PAY *lets* LAURE *go.*)

LAURE: I'm not going to let you, Pay. I'm not going to allow you to force me to say what I don't mean to say!

LAURE: Then outsmart me. Say what you really mean. Tell me what's really going on. Make a fool out of me and my paranoid suspicions. *(Yelling)* NO! You can't, can you? You're afraid to say what's really going on, because you might end up jeopardizing what's most important to you—your relationship to him!

LAURE: That's not true!

PAY: Of course it is. I may be a bit shaky these days, but I know what's true. Do you know Bunuel's movie, the one where they slice open an eye with a razor?

LAURE: I've heard of it.

PAY: See, what Bunuel is doing, in his masterly way, is telling us to look at the world with our inner eye— like surrealists and madmen do. But, you see, I'm not qualified to be a surrealist. I haven't done the proper preparation. But the madman thing I have sewed up. I could pass any type of madman test they threw at me. *(He begins to get lost here.)* You see, someone told me about this inner eye stuff, but I can't remember exactly who, for the life of me, I just can't manage it… Some violent inconsolable, I imagine. Though I think it's a great concept. Going right to the heart of the matter, even existence. If only you have the guts to keep looking at the horror screaming at your feet. But of course, nobody can do that for very long. Can they?

LAURE: Pay, sit down. Try and relax.

PAY: No! Don't try and take me out of my game! Remember, I'm not only nuts, but dangerous as well!

Spear knows all about the dangerous part. That's why he wants me—wants to harness my cheap energy! Use it as a potent force of social retardation! And you know what the pathetic truth is: something in me wouldn't kind'a mind so much if he did. I mean, why not just go with him, run around, kill elephants, blow things up! Who cares? As long as you can rock the world off its orbit for a second or two—make them pay attention to what you lost—and how pissed off you are about it! So they take you out, so what? As long as you had a few laughs. I mean, fuck them if they can't take a joke! *(He laughs.)* But I won't—I don't think—do it. I don't know exactly why, but I just won't. I just know I have to stand my ground. As long as I can, anyway. As if there was some purpose to it—which I'm confused about. And probably don't believe in, anyway.

LAURE: *(She goes to him)* Pay, no more. I'm sorry. I really am, saying the things I said. If I hurt you, I… *(She touches his face. He pulls away.)*

PAY: Don't be sorry. Just tell me the truth.

LAURE: You know something, Pay. I'm afraid you really don't want to hear my truth. You only want me to say what you want to hear. So tell me: what is it you really want me to say?

PAY: I want you to say, that what you really want to be is a martyr. That you want to go up in flames, like Joan of Arc. Maybe in the center of town, with everybody watching—like Joan of Arc before the television cameras—because your life has been emptied of meaning. Can you say that, Laure? But in your own words.

LAURE: No. Because I don't want to be a martyr. What I want to do is something significant! Is that so wrong? Does that make me evil?

PAY: No. But you're going about it the wrong way, and with the wrong person. Why don't you smarten up, Laure?

LAURE: You know, I think you're really jealous of him. It keeps coming down to that, doesn't it?

PAY: Oh, yeah? Tell me about it.

LAURE: Because he can think and he can act.

PAY: And you don't think I can, right? Too far gone, too fucking nuts for thinking and acting in a coherent manner. All I'm good for is becoming some sort of slave to his will. But you know what: even if what you think about me is true—I'm still following something, Laure—even if I don't know exactly what it is or if it'll get me out of this terrible situation I'm in, but still I'm…

LAURE: So is he following something, Pay!

PAY: Don't make me laugh! Superman? Nitroman? Look! The Flaming ego lighting up the sky! Shield your eyes, 'cause he might blind you! But not me; I've got special eyes. We were nine years old together! There are no surprises.

LAURE: He needs to believe in himself, in order to get things done. Why can't you see that? Why can't *you* believe in that?

PAY: He's gone over the edge. He's got weapons. He's ready to use them. And you know what, he thinks what he's doing is notable, is somehow beatific!

LAURE: I don't know about weapons.

PAY: But I know.

LAURE: I don't care.

PAY: That's great, Laure! Finally something truthful out of you. Now you said it, finally said it. So what's the use of me worrying about you, thinking about you, caring about you, anymore? You can go to hell!

LAURE: I love him! I love what he thinks, and what he does, and what he believes! And I love his courage!

PAY: My courage doesn't count, though, does it? Because it's the courage of a murderer, and beneath contempt to someone as moral and upright as you!

LAURE: I never said that. I never thought that.

PAY: You thought it, one way or another. Do you love him as a man?

LAURE: I love him for what he is, and what he's trying to do.

PAY: You once loved me as a man.

LAURE: Yes, I did.

PAY: Do you still love me that way?

LAURE: I…don't…know. What you don't seem to understand, Pay, it's not just you that's suffering. This is a time of great uncertainty, great suffering for all of us; and my soul reflects that pain. Though I'm trying not to show it; not so much for the world, but for myself. Because, like him, I need to believe in myself in order to keep going. That's all I can say now.

PAY: But that's not enough. I'm disappointed. Say something else.

LAURE: Please leave me alone now, Pay. I'm tired.

PAY: You see, I'm home now; I'm home from the wars. Doesn't anybody know what that means?

LAURE: What does it mean?

PAY: It means the bullshit's ended! It's finally over for me! And now I have to make things straight. No matter what! No matter who it takes down! Because I gotta make some sense out of the mess I'm in! Or, or… And you know something, I don't really want to think about that last 'or' of mine.

LAURE: I'm afraid we're trapped in two different worlds, Pay, without any hope of connecting.

PAY: Yeah, sure. But I'm not going away, yet. *(He is looking around the room. He sees a pile of papers sitting on a table.)* What do you got over there, homework?

(PAY sees the fear in LAURE's eyes, and moves quickly, grabbing the papers.)

LAURE: Hey! You have no right to touch those!

(PAY starts to read the papers. LAURE tries to get them away from him, he shoves her back. She tries again, and he shoves her back even harder.)

LAURE: Give it over, Pay!

PAY: His stuff, huh?

LAURE: His notes, yes. I'm just putting them in order. Now give them back!

PAY: *(Reading)* Who does he think he is, Martin Luther? What's he planning to do, tack these to the fucking door of the White House! *(He starts to rip them up.)* When I get finished he'll need a thousand tacks to do the job!

(LAURE rushes PAY. He raises his hand.)

LAURE: You'd really hit me, Pay?

PAY: Just try me!

LAURE: Go ahead then, soldier! Do anything you want! Get it over with! Because, you know what: now I know what you're really about! What you're really like! What you're really up to! You're on the job, aren't you? On the prowl! Hunting down those little red commie bastards! Tracking them right into their pathetic

hooches! Ready and willing to give them just what
they goddamn deserve!

(PAY *stops ripping the papers and stares at* LAURE.)

LAURE: What's the matter, got taken out of your game?
Afraid of paper cuts? That's too bad. Maybe you need
some help? Hey, how about a lighter? I have a nice
Zippo stashed somewhere. A nice big shiny lighter. U
S issue. Throws a big fat flame! Able to burn up those
Commie Red words easy as pie! How about it, soldier?
It's yours for the asking!

PAY: Good, Laure! Good, good, good! You've finally
said what you really mean! You've said it all now!
The mystery's gone! Everything's cleared up! Now I
know exactly what you think of me! Feel about me! I'm
impressed! You've given the truth game your best shot!
More than I ever expected.

(PAY *begins tearing the papers and hurling pieces at* LAURE.
She covers herself, wincing as if bits of fire were hitting her.)

PAY: Thanks, Laure. Thanks a lot. My best girl! My
soul mate! Fellow sexual adventurer! Old and steadfast
friend! Thanks.

LAURE: Stop it, Pay. Please… Everything's breaking
down. Words coming out wild and wrong and…
unforgivable…Pay…

PAY: No! They're coming out first rate. Your words,
anyway. (*He finishes throwing the last of the paper.*) And
now, Laure, there's something I need to tell you—
because I haven't finished yet, haven't said what I
needed to say about your life, your future. And I think
it's important—even though I know you think I'm a
piece of shit, and most everything I say is worthless.
But still, Laure, still… If you're not careful, you're
going to end up suffering big time, for aiding and
abetting, conspiracy—and God knows what else! And

remember, there are people out there eager to get their hands on you, eager to make an example of you, to dig their patriotic claws into your flesh—and when they finish with your public torture, they're gonna put you away! For years, Laure! Think of it: years going by— but slow, slow, and mean, and unforgiving—dragging everything good out of you, the beauty of your youth, the light of your eyes, your lovely skin. But the worst of it is, that someday you're going to realize what you've done had little value. That you've not only wasted your idealism, but defiled it as well. But by then it'll be too late—because nobody's going to have any pity for you—and Spear will probably be dead, or doing harder time than you—and I'll be long gone— and God knows what I'll think, if I'm around to think, when the thought of you crosses my mind. Did you hear me, Laure?

LAURE: You want to kill me, don't you?

PAY: No. What I want to kill is what's killing you!

LAURE: You're as bad as him! The two of you are alike! You'll do anything you can to get what you want! Each of you playing me against the other! Playing me against myself! My two male heroes! What a lucky girl I am!

PAY: Do you really believe that? I mean… Is that what's going on? Is that what we're doing? *(He tries to touch her face.)*

LAURE: Don't touch me, Pay!

PAY: All right, all right. I won't—ever again. *(He starts backing away from her, when he starts to sense an explosion approaching him—similar to the one he experienced with the hand grenade—zeroing in on him. About to engulf him)*

LAURE: Pay, what's the matter?

PAY: I can't help it. What's happening... Anything...at all... I cant.

(It takes him now, engulfing and shattering him. He falls to his knees. A muffled explosion.)

LAURE: Pay! *(She starts to move towards him.)*

(Darkness. The lights come up dim, early morning. PAY *stands there. He looks dishevelled, beat up. But there is a slight smile on his face.)*

PAY: A couple of guys jumped me the other night. I was out alone, roaming the city. Drinking in some of the seedier bars. First there was one of them, it seemed, then maybe two. Then who knows, maybe three coming at me. I couldn't get a good look at any of them. I couldn't tell where it began or ended. But in the midst of it, I found myself excited—happy, even. A well trained fighter/killer. Everything on the line. Good to hurt, and be hurt, if need be. To run, to hide, to ambush. Then all of a sudden they were gone. And I just stood there... The sun starting to make its move across the river. And right above me, two stars just hanging there, waiting for me to look up—very low, very mysterious; closer than I had ever seen stars before.

(At this point we see SPEAR *standing in the shadows.)*

SPEAR: Welcome back, Pay. To the place where you belong; to the land of the living; the land of exhilaration. Of vigorous exultation.

PAY: *(Hearing him but trying to ignore him; a slight smile on his face. To the audience.)* Hey, listen, I almost forget the great part. This! *(He holds up a wallet.)* I found it on the ground after the donnybrook had run its course. One of theirs? I don't know. There was no identification. But there was money. A good deal of money; at least by my standards.

(PAY *smiles, turns and starts to walk away. The light comes up. Morning. He turns around, smiling at the audience.*)

PAY: It was a beautiful day; a lucky day, for sure. I decided to go to the track. I got there just in time for the fourth race. My friend Wendell was already there; he wasn't doing very well. Don't worry, Wendell, I said, stick with me. Because today, bro, I've got the magic. I was studying the racing form. It looked good to me. Very good, actually. Lots of strangely compelling names began jumping out at me. It took me only a few seconds to realize what I had to do. Wendell thought I was crazy. He had never heard of a bet like mine in his life! But something about my certainty must have convinced him, because he decided to risk his last twenty bucks. And there they go! How I love it! The smell of the place, the horse shit, the beer, the smoke—the wheelers and dealers, the high flyers and the low dippers—the broads and the touts right out of Damon Runyon—and perched on the backs of the monsters, their diminutive masters—caught up in an explosion of turf and hooves, danger and speed— helmeted madmen riding the sacred edge of panic! And the crowd collectively unzipped!— naked and mad and screaming! Come on, come on, I'm yelling! Come on Danag, come on Kontum, Dak To, Ia Drang, come on Khe Sanh, come on Citadel City! They're coming into the stretch now, neck and neck! —and then an incredible thing happens-it's a photo finish! And after a few minutes the results are posted—and believe it or not!—they all won! Every one of them! Wendell and me began hugging and kissing each other like a couple of maniacs! It turns out I have so much money that they have to stick it into a couple of canvas bags! But coming home on the train, a strange thing happens—the bags begin dripping something. Drops of blood, it turns out. The bags are dripping blood all

over the train! Pretty soon everybody is looking at me,
as if I had done something horrible; as if I were some
kind of a murderer. I decide I'll leave the bags and get
off the train! Just forget them! But I can't. I couldn't—
because they belonged to me! To me! Because they
were part of me somehow! By the time I left the train
the floor was slick with blood. But I did not drop the
bags. I did not leave them behind.

(SPEAR *is standing in the shadows watching him. Darkness.
The lights come up on* PAY'*s apartment. He comes out of the
bedroom. He had been sleeping, but has been awakened by a
noise. Now he hears hears something again.)*

PAY: Hey! Who's there?

SPEAR: I didn't hear anything.

PAY: What? What the hell's going on?

SPEAR: *(Pops up from behind the couch. He is wearing a
Bugs Bunny mask.)* What's up, Doc?

PAY: What? I mean… You wascally wabbit!

SPEAR: I got'cha now, Doc!

(SPEAR *laugh, then pulls out a gun and points it at* PAY.)

PAY: What's up, Rabbit? Why the hardware?

(SPEAR *starts laughing and shooting at* PAY. *The gun is
a water pistol.* PAY *starts laughing—trying to block the
squirts. Now* SPEAR *tosses* PAY *a pistol and they begin
laughing and shooting at each other—running around the
room like a couple of wild kids. Finally they stop.)*

SPEAR: *(In his Bug's voice)* Help me out, will ya, Doc?

PAY: What's up, Bugs?

SPEAR: You see, what it is, Doc, what's got me
stymied—I'm not really Bugs. But find myself trapped
by him, for illicit purposes, no less. So help me, Doc!
Because this wascally rabbit, is in truth, a wascally

bandit of a rodent! *(Panicking)* Please help me, Doc! *(He grabs hold of the mask and begins trying to pull it off.)*

PAY: Easy, easy, whoever you are! We'll take care of that bad rabbit once and for all!

(Now both of them begin struggling with the mask, until finally, after a mighty effort, they tear it off, throw it to the ground, and then begin shooting it with their water pistols.)

(Blackout. The lights come back up. SPEAR takes out a bottle of Jack Daniels and offers it to PAY.)

PAY: You want us to drink?

SPEAR: That's the idea.

PAY: The two of us?

SPEAR: Yup.

PAY: You think that's wise?

SPEAR: No, I don't.

PAY: Well, in that case… *(He takes the bottle and drinks.)*

(Blackout. The lights come up. PAY and SPEAR show the effects of the alcohol but are not drunk.)

PAY: So tell me, why exactly did you go holy on us?

SPEAR: I can't believe I never told you why.

PAY: Some of it, but not all of it.

SPEAR: You mean, what really drove me into that monastery for a year and a half?

PAY: Yeah. The whole story.

SPEAR: The truth is, it was some kind of crazy mental experiment—seeing that, unlike most of the men in residence, I did not believe in God—as you know. *(He smiles.)* But somehow I wanted to be in an atmosphere conducive to the experience of religion.

PAY: So did you manage to have some kind of a religious experience?

SPEAR: In a cockeyed sort of way, I did.

PAY: What kind of experience was it?

SPEAR: What happened is, well, I decided to try and create God.

PAY: Oh, I get it. Start off with the easy stuff.

SPEAR: That's right. But I kind of reversed it a bit.

PAY: What do you mean?

PAY: Instead of God making us like Him, I decided to make Him like me—in my image and likeness, is what I'm saying. And it wasn't easy. It took hundreds and hundreds of hours of silence and contemplation, not to mention, mental and physical agony, before I was able to bring it off.

PAY: And what did you want from this God of yours?

SPEAR: Power.

PAY: Did He come across for you?

SPEAR: Eventually. But it wasn't easy. What you had to do is, to get Him to want to give it to you.

PAY: How'd you manage that, bribery?

SPEAR: Yeah, Sort of. You see, you have to love Him, give Him attention; your best stuff, I'm talking about— if you want something from Him in return. The truth is, He thrives on painful sacrifices and spiritual excesses. And when you give Him enough, and if you're lucky—He might give you what you want in return—in my case, power.

PAY: And is that what He did?

SPEAR: Yes.

PAY: And how much did He give you?

SPEAR: As much as I could handle; which is a lot.

PAY: You know what? I think I'd like to change the conversation.

SPEAR: Why's that?

PAY: Because a human being cannot be God! A human being can only be what he is! Only insane Roman emperors think they're gods!

SPEAR: But a human of great dedication and superior intellect, can sometimes project himself to the nth degree, with the results being next to godlike.

PAY: That's bullshit!

(SPEAR *laughs.*)

PAY: What's so funny?

SPEAR: The expression on your face! All that anger and contempt flaring up in you! It's like the old days! My man! After all these years and you're still my man! Nothing can change that! (*He continues laughing.*)

PAY: I'm not your man, asshole!

SPEAR: So I suffer from an overload of pride—what would you like me to do—cut off my head?

PAY: Do what you want. Just leave me out of it.

SPEAR: Don't worry, Pay, the God experiment is now over. Somehow I lost Him; I couldn't sustain Him. He gave me a lot; He carried me a long way. I thought I'd have Him around forever; but one day it all changed. A case of spiritual leprosy, I guess. Every time I tried to conjure him up, He'd start to fall apart in front of me: His eyes, His intellect, His heart, His mouth, His balls, whatever, until He was completely gone. I was bereft. I had nothing to fall back on; nothing to believe in. Until…

PAY: (*Cutting him off*) Until you decided to go back to your past, to your glory days—to you and me and Laure, as we were in our innocence—because we had

no idea of what we would become in our weakness—
or how little we mattered in the scheme of things—-
back to those days when everything we wanted was
everywhere—and all we had to do was to reach out
and take it—and we were happy.

SPEAR: You're a smart guy, Pay. Smarter than you
deserve, I sometimes think.

PAY: What do you mean by that?

SPEAR: Don't worry about it, Pay. It's just a fact, just a
mere fact.

PAY: Fuck you. Fuck you again and again!

SPEAR: Yes, again and again! Because we're strapped to
a wheel, pal! The two of us! And somehow neither one
of us has found a way to get off! So we revolve—we
fucking revolve!

*(Blackout. The lights come back up, The men are slumped in
chairs on opposite sides of the room.* PAY *and* SPEAR *have
continued drinking. They each have glass with whiskey in it
next to them. The alcohol has taken more effect.)*

SPEAR: So why'd you do it?

PAY: I told you. I was drafted.

SPEAR: That's not much of answer, is it?

PAY: Tell me, why should I tell you anything?

SPEAR: Because this is a primal visit, Pay. The one
where we settle things and go on together or end it…
decisively. So I want to get all the facts straight, before
we go on to part two.

PAY: End it! That's terrific. That's good news. You've
given me an incentive. A worthwhile goal. You wantta
hear what happened? Then listen.

SPEAR: I'm all ears. I used to be a rabbit, you know.

PAY: You see, My father had a trick knee—he didn't make that up, but he coddled it a bit, then went limping down to the draft board with his wobbly crutches and got himself a 4F. It didn't really matter, though; because a month later my mother got pregnant with my older brother, and he would have got a deferment, anyway. *(He drinks.)* You know, I met guys who went on starvation diets so as to turn themselves into anemics, who took pills to turn their urine purple, guys who came to their physical wearing women's underwear, others who went to anti-war psychiatrists who wrote statements saying that under no circumstances should this man be allowed to serve in the American army—not to mention, the dudes who want to Canada and Mexico, and God knows where else to start a new life. And I never hated those men, whatever they did was their personal agenda, so let them follow it. But it just wasn't in me to do something like that. It wasn't a war I particularly liked; but it was a war my country was involved in, and a lot of guys like me were doing the fighting, some of them dying— so I went.

SPEAR: That's bullshit.

PAY: What?

SPEAR: Just the surface of things. You haven't gotten anywhere near real or said anything of value. Give it another try.

PAY: I thought we were going to end it tonight.

SPEAR: Sure. But we haven't got there yet. When we get there, you'll know it. Believe me. *(A beat)* Gunga Din.

PAY: What? What did you say?

SPEAR: Your poem. They one you forced us to recite day after day, for God knows how long. Don't you remember?

PAY: I'm afraid not. (*His world starts to come apart a bit.*)

SPEAR: Now in Injia's sunny clime,
Where I used to spend my time
A-servin' of 'Er Majesty the Queen,
Of all them black-faced crew
The finest man I knew
Was our regimental bhisti, Gunga Din.
Remember that, Pay?

PAY: No.

SPEAR: It was "Din! Din! Din!
You limping lump o'brick-dust, Gunga Din!
Hi! slippy hitherao!
Water, get it! PANEE LAO!
You squidgy-nosed old idol, Gunga Din!"
That's what you wanted, wasn't it, Pay? A chance to
redeem yourself through heroic self sacrifice!

PAY: That's bullshit!

SPEAR: Your father used to treat you like shit. Don't
you remember? Nothing you did amounted to
anything, as far as he was concerned. As hard as you
tried, it was useless. We all saw it; you ignored it.

PAY: Sometimes he was a pain in the ass, sure
(*He is struggling to get himself back on track, but not
making it.*) But he wasn't so bad. NOT SO BAD YOU
UNDERSTAND! UNDERSTAND HE WAS HE! HIS
ATTITUDE WAS HIS! AND I WAS NOT HIM! EVER
HIM! FORGET HIM! BECAUSE I WASN'T HIM!
WHO CARED? NEVER HIM! UNDERSTAND? WHO
CARED! NOT ME! FUCK IT!

SPEAR: You cared.

PAY: NO! HE WASN'T ME YOU UNDERSTAND! HE
WAS OTHER! HIS RIGHT! WHO CARED? NOBODY!

SPEAR: So you became Gunga Din. The blackest of
the black, the lowest of the low—hoping to transform
yourself HEROICALLY in battle! Your father, who
was practically a draft dodger, would end up looking
pathetic next to you. You'd come home a hero—
either shiny with medals, or wrapped in a body-
bag—whatever; because it really didn't make much
difference, now did it? Since whatever happened,
you'd still be greater than him.

PAY: Not true! That, that's…ERROR! ERROR!

*(The scene breaks down; PAY breaks down. Darkness. The
lights come up. PAY is slumped in a chair. SPEAR is sitting
on the other side of the room watching him.)*

PAY: You know what it was, what nobody knows…
Because things creep up on you. And then you push
them back down. Deeper in. And then nobody hears
anything. Deeper in. So far that nobody can hear a
thing. Nothing, not a word. Even the hearer hears
nothing. Only silence. Because nobody wants to know
the truth. Because… A few days after Charlie Chop
got it… This patrol I'm in surprises a bunch of them.
Shoots them up pretty bad. And then, what nobody
knows… One of them comes running out of the trees.
But soldier boy's got…got…got the drop on him. So
he, he…throws down his weapon, and ups his hands!
And, I swear, says: American! Hey, American! Rock'n
roll! Chuck Berry, Little Richard! Long life Rock 'n
roll! Long life! And then soldier boy, solider boy…
Soldier boy shoots him dead in the chest! Shoots him!
No problem there. Just shoots him dead! Just like that.
Even though he's…he's a big…a big rock 'n roll fan!
But you know what, I don't ever remember seeing him
hanging around the fucking Paramount. Do you ever
remember seeing that little Viet Cong bastard hanging
around? Bo Diddley, Little Richard, Screaming Jay
Hawkins, you remember them—but not him!

(After a few long moments SPEAR *begins to laugh.)*

PAY: What? Who are you laughing at? What's so funny?

SPEAR: *(Laughing)* Correct me if I'm wrong: You go to war to redeem yourself, to make yourself holy, in quest of some nobility, and...

PAY: Fuck that! I didn't do that!

SPEAR: And what do you end up becoming? —a psychotic killer, a demented cowboy! Only a complete asshole would let himself go like you did—wig out and blast some defenseless rock 'n roll loving, commie, peasant kid to death for the hell of it!

PAY: *(Stands up)* Shut up! Shut up! *(He has a gun in his hand, one of the water pistols.)*

SPEAR: Boy, did they do a job on you!

*(*PAY *starts squirting him in the face.)*

SPEAR: Turning you into a abject murderer! Removing what was left of the moral center of your brain! Not to mention your heart! *(He continues laughing, but at the same time tries to block the water with his hands.)*

PAY: *(Still shooting)* What's a matter, tough guy! Can't take a little water? A little water is all it is—all it takes to turn you into a cringing rat! Maybe you're afraid you're going to shrink back down into that squeaking, little nothing that you truly are?

SPEAR: *(Laughing)* A clown, a lunatic, a butcher! No wonder you're fucked up! Funniest thing I ever heard! What a hero! Maybe you'll get a medal for it? Get Elvis to pin it on! *(He drops his hands. We see that he's furious.)* Keep shooting, man! Keep shooting! You wantta keep shooting, is that it? So keep on shooting!

PAY: Oh, we're getting a reaction no, aren't we? Seems that old God of vengeance is back on full throttle!

(SPEAR *pulls out a gun and points it at* PAY. *It is obviously real.*)

PAY: I don't care what you're pointing at me! You understand?

(PAY *continues shooting until his gun runs out of water.* PAY *and* SPEAR *stand there, guns pointed at each other.*)

PAY: Now what are we going to do? Come on! Come up with something, moron! Do something! Because, you know what? —Nothing bothers me now, especially you!

(*Darkness. The lights come up.* PAY *and* SPEAR *are sitting in chairs on opposite sides of the room, sipping their drinks.*)

SPEAR: Let me tell you what the plan is, what's going to happen. We're going to finish it now. Okay? Our relationship, I'm talking about. Totally. For good. 'Cause it takes two to Tango. You understand? And we're desperate men, each in our own way. You agree?

PAY: I agree.

SPEAR: So does it sound good to you?

PAY: Sounds perfect. How we gonna go about it?

(SPEAR *gets up, and goes to the middle of the room, then puts the gun, the real one, down on the floor.*)

SPEAR: The Runaway Boys. The first one gets it does the deed. First we get equidistant. Then we go for it. No chickening out. It's a matter of pride. Of honor. Of brotherhood. What else do we have, I mean? Nothing, when you think about it. Because everything else, we've either lost or given away or had stolen from us. You get it?

PAY: Sure. I get it.

SPEAR: Good. You know, in Cuba, I found out something early on: Castro was El Jefe, but Che, Che was God. Guess who I wanted to be?

PAY: I have no idea.

SPEAR: *(Laughing)* What I absolutely did not want, you see, was to become like one of those dried out, soulless, Marxist/Leninists little shits, slinking around college campuses, browbeating people with their pretentious theories—hopeless little termites gnawing away at a country that was much too powerful for them to take on in the first place, let alone digest—instead of coming up with a greatness of their own. But somehow, each day, I find myself drifting in their direction; unable to sufficiently resist—like I'm being dragged out to sea by some slow moving current—unable to find what I need. Or what I really want. Bankrupt, but not yet completely corrupt. *(He laughs,)* So you see, I need to set things straight.

PAY: You really think this is the answer?

SPEAR: Not so much an answer, but a major step that needs to be taken—unless…

PAY: Unless, what?

SPEAR: Unless we're able to get the Runaway Boys back together again.

PAY: You know, I just don't think that's going to happen.

SPEAR: All right. I see you've made up your mind. That's fine. No problem. I respect that. So…

PAY: *(Interrupting him)* What happens if I refuse to participate?

SPEAR: I'm afraid that would not be a wise position to take.

PAY: I know when you're serious, and I know when you're insane. And now, it seems, you're both.

SPEAR: *(Smiling)* Nothing to be ashamed of about that! So let us commence.

(PAY *puts the gun down on the floor in the middle of the room. The two men count an equal distance and remain standing there.* SPEAR *begins to silently count, illustrating each number with his fingers: one, two, and then, he yells "three." They race to the gun.)*

(Blackout. A short fierce struggle. When the lights come up, SPEAR *is sitting down drinking.* PAY *is standing up, pointing the gun at him.)*

SPEAR: You've already taken too long. I have nothing but contempt for your lack of action. It's not only irritating, it's sickening. No wonder you have problems getting from A to B. No wonder you have trouble figuring out who's alive and who's dead. It seems there's no pride or guts or intelligence left inside you.

PAY: What about Laure?

SPEAR: She's alive, last I heard.

PAY: I'm not talking about that. I'm talking about what's going to happen to her when you're gone?

SPEAR: Laure can take care of herself.

PAY: You're the one made the mess, and then she's left with it?

SPEAR: She's peripheral. She's not important. And I resent the word "mess".

PAY: So now she's a nothing, a nobody.

SPEAR: I didn't say that. You're the one said that.

PAY: It seems you get to take the easy way out.

SPEAR: *(Suddenly smiling)* Hey, Pay, don't tell me—but are you still in love with her? I mean, I thought those adolescent crushes were long gone.

PAY: I just want things to be fair—for her to have a chance to lead her own life—not be saddled with your mistakes.

ACT TWO   87

SPEAR: Then I guess she didn't tell you?

PAY: What?

SPEAR: I told her that she should tell you.

PAY: Tell me what? What are you talking about?

SPEAR: That we've been lovers for over a year. It's only fair I said, let him know what's going on.

(PAY *looks stricken.*)

SPEAR: You see, what happened, she tried hard to keep her love and respect for you intact—no matter how horrible the situation was over there—no matter what she imagined you were doing—but eventually she just couldn't take it anymore. Things started falling apart in her mind. In other words, she needed other outlets, other viewpoints, other men. I mean, a serious relationship, not some diversionary little affair. *(He stares at* PAY's *face and then starts to laugh.)* Go ahead, you cuckolded little fuck! Be a man! That's it! Go ahead! Assert yourself! Get even! Do what you...

(PAY *hits* SPEAR *with butt of the gun, knocking him to the floor.)*

(Blackout. The lights come up. PAY *is sitting on a chair, pointing the gun at* SPEAR, *who is sitting on the floor, holding his jaw.)*

SPEAR: What a shot! *(He is feeling around in his mouth with his hand and tongue.)* Well, I guess all my teeth are still in their rightful places. One's a little wobbly, though. Hey, I'm sorry about that cuckold thing. I shouldn't have said it. It was nasty. I apologize.

PAY: What about Laure? What's going to happen to her?

SPEAR: She's a innocent. She knows nothing. She can't be implicated.

PAY: Still, they'll go after her.

SPEAR: Hey! You're worried, because you love her! Isn't that right? Am I correct? I mean, it's not just jealousy, is it? You still love her, because you've always loved her, and you'll continue to love her—no matter what she does or thinks about you. Interesting, isn't it?

PAY: What's so interesting about it?

SPEAR: I don't know. Just is. To me, anyway. Your dedication to someone—without any strings attached. How do you manage it?

PAY: Get out of here. I don't want to talk to you anymore. I don't want to see you anymore. Understand? *(He gets up, goes over to a table, and places the gun on top of it.)* Just go.

SPEAR: You shouldn't have done that.

PAY: Who cares? It's done.

SPEAR: You broke the rules! It was a big mistake! I don't like being treated like an asshole! My plans are important to me! My word is important to me! I base real ideas, real actions on what I think—on what I've promised myself to do! Not like other people, who just muddle along, mouthing and complaining their fucking lives away! *(He gets up and goes over to the gun, but does not pick it up.)* So, tell me. Who else have you loved in this world of yours? Anybody of note?

PAY: I don't know. What's the difference?

SPEAR: You loved your mother, didn't you?

PAY: Yeah. A lot.

SPEAR: And what about your father?

PAY: I gave him his due.

SPEAR: Anybody else?

PAY: I don't know. Yeah. There was this kid I used to hang out with when we were young. This crazy kid.

We were always together. I guess it was a kind of love.
As strong as any, I would think, when you think back
on it.

SPEAR: So what did the two of you to do together?

PAY: Oh, I don't know. Lots of stuff, you know.

SPEAR: Tell me about it. Something specific that you'd
do together.

PAY: Well, when we around ten or so, all the kids we
hung out with were into making these contraptions
called pushcarts. I don't know why we called them
that, because you didn't really push them, but rode
them instead. Anyway, what we'd do is to sneak over
to a construction site—there were always lots of them
around in those days—and steal a two-by-four. Then
we'd take it home and saw it in half, and get an old
pair of roller skates and nail them on to the bottom of
the two by four. Then we'd get one of those wooden
boxes that they used to ship fruits and vegetables in,
and nail it to the top of the board. And then to finish it
off, we'd get a couple of pieces of wood and nail them
in a V shape to the top of the box to use for steering.

SPEAR: Then what would you do with it?

PAY: Well, me and my buddy and a couple of other
kids from the neighborhood would go over to this big
hill over where I used to live. And when it was clear
of traffic, we'd push off in our fragile contraptions.
And then, like little demons, we'd start racing down
the hill. Each of us trying to get to the intersection first.
And sometimes, you know, it would get pretty hairy
going down so fast—what with traffic barrelling down
at you from behind—and the drivers honking their
horns and screaming—you little bastards, get off the
road! And the stupid pushcarts shaking and shattering
with every bump and rut and crevice. And at that
point me and my buddy would sometimes look at each

other, and start howling with fear and laughter. And when we'd hit the intersection—even though we knew what we were doing was nuts—we wouldn't stop or slow down for a second—not for anybody!—but go right through—as if it was our God given right! Little demons, laughing and howling, forcing the rest of the world to slam on their goddamn brakes, so that we could pass through!

(PAY begins to laugh wildly. SPEAR howls a terrible howl, then grabbing the gun, points it at PAY. Blackout. A gunshot. The lights come up. PAY is standing there. SPEAR is gone.)

PAY: He fired the gun into the wall and then hit me with it. Wanted to make up for the wallop I gave him, I guess. I felt terrible; not so much my head, but my heart. I felt that I had let him down; that I hadn't played by the rules. I felt sick inside. He was probably right about me; I couldn't follow through on anything, could I? I was useless. But then I thought about it some more, and began to feel that I had been set up. Spear was strong. I had wrestled with him enough in the past to know that. How come I got the gun away from him so easily? He had it first, tight in his hand—and then I had it. Just like that. How come? Because he was setting me up, that's how come. I had two choices: either do the deed, or bring the Runaway boys back together. But neither one of those things was something I could bring myself to do. But then he got hold of the gun and was forced to deal with the same dilemma. But he couldn't handle it, either. As much as he wanted to bring it off, as much as he tried, he couldn't. The truth being, he thought he really needed to do something significant, life altering, in order to go on and lead the life he felt was his destiny to live. But still, he just could not do what he needed to do. I think he viewed his inability to act as a terrible weakness.

When he walked out of the room he must have seen
himself as a failure—something new and horrible to
him; something totally unacceptable to him. Soon after
that I went to visit my mother. They were right about
her or partly right, anyway; she was gone. I mean,
she wasn't there in her physical presence. But still, I
felt very sad and helpless, standing in the middle of
the nowhere where I once lived. But after a while, I
started to brighten up, as the good memories came
flooding back: the parties, the fun, the music we used
to play down in the basement. I guess I went a little
bit topsy turvy that night: turning on all the lights,
playing music as loud I could, diving into the bottle
of Seagrams I found in the usual cabinet. But then,
in the midst of the festivities, a couple of cops came
knocking at the door. It was two a.m. The neighbors
must have called them. I let them in, even offered them
a drink, but things didn't work out very well. Soon
words started to fly, and then fists. I knocked the fat
one down. The other one came at me with his club in
the air, his face bursting with beet red hatred. And
that's when I cried out—at the top of my lungs—at the
pitch black top of the night where all the stars are dead
and nothing moves: I'm a veteran of an American war!
(He cries this out, and then, softly…) I'm a veteran of an
American war.

(The lights go dark, then slowly begin to grow brighter.)

PAY: They put me in the psych ward of an upstate
V A hospital. But it wasn't so bad. Nobody really
bothered me much. Nobody fucked with me all that
much. I guess they saw my fatigue for what it was:
a deep and lonely thing, an unnamed animal that
needed to be left alone. And that's what they pretty
much did. One day, though, one of the nurses gave me
a book to read: Homer's story about the Trojan War.
I read it very carefully; soon realizing that not much

had changed, if anything, in so many thousands of years—what with the terrible battles men are forced to fight—what they rise to, and what they sink under; what happens to their minds and spirits in the midst of it all—not to mention when its over, grasping at ashes and memories for solace; the half wind speaking to them in unknown tongues. Half way through the book I read in the papers that Spear was dead. He had been living in a cheap apartment in the Mission District in San Francisco, with a couple of his buddies. It seems they were about ready to hit a military installation. Blew himself up, they said. He was alone when it happened. He must have got careless, they said. Bullshit, I said! Spear get careless with wires and charges and explosives? Ha! He could have brought that off half asleep as a twelve year old kid! *(He laughs a little.)* Because, the thing is: Spear always did exactly what he wanted to do. There were very few accidents when it came to him. *(Pause.)* I kept reading the papers to see if there was anything about Laure. There wasn't. But then, out of the blue, I found myself speaking to someone from the neighborhood who knew her family well. And he told me that, yes, they had gone after her—labelling her a disloyal American, a reckless and dangerous person who would stop at nothing in order to destroy the war effort. But she got herself a very good lawyer, and before long the matter was dropped, for lack of evidence. He also heard that she was fired from her job, and had decided to leave the country. But he had no idea where she was going or when she was leaving. A couple of weeks later I was discharged from the hospital. One day I decided to call her up, for old time's sake, I guess. *(He looks around him.)* It wasn't a beautiful day; actually it was a grey and drizzly day.

(We now see LAURE *standing in the little park down by the river. She is looking out at the water, her back to* PAY.*)*

PAY: I almost left; I did; I swear. I almost lost my nerve. When, when…

LAURE: *(Turns around)* Pay! It's so good to see you! It really is!

(PAY *begins walking towards* LAURE.)

END OF PLAY

www.ingramcontent.com/pod-product-compliance
Lightning Source LLC
Chambersburg PA
CBHW052157090426
42741CB00010B/2302